Worship Planning
Resources for
Every Sunday of the Year

The Abingdon Worship Annual 2026

Edited by
Mary Scifres
and B. J. Beu

Abingdon Press / Nashville

THE ABINGDON WORSHIP ANNUAL 2026:
WORSHIP PLANNING RESOURCES
FOR EVERY SUNDAY OF THE YEAR

Copyright © 2025 by Abingdon Press

All rights reserved.
Prayers, litanies, and other worship resources in this book may be reproduced by local church congregations, except where noted by individual copyright, provided the following credit line and copyright notice appear on all copies: "From *The Abingdon Worship Annual 2026*. Copyright © 2025 by Abingdon Press. Used by permission." Individual copyright notice should accompany all copies of material covered by individual copyright. No other part of this work may be reproduced or transmitted in any form or by any means, electronic or mechanical, including photocopying and recording, or by any information storage or retrieval system, except as may be expressly permitted by the 1976 Copyright Act, the 1998 Digital Millennium Copyright Act, or in writing from the publisher. Requests for permission should be addressed to Abingdon Press, 810 12th Avenue South, Nashville, TN or emailed to permissions@abingdonpress.com.

ISBN 978-1-7910-3803-8

All lectionary verses and all Scripture quotations, unless noted otherwise, are taken from the Common English Bible (CEB), copyright 2011. Used by permission. All rights reserved.

Scripture quotations marked NRSVUE are taken from the New Revised Standard Version Updated Edition. Copyright © 2021 National Council of Churches of Christ in the United States of America. Used by permission. All rights reserved worldwide.

MANUFACTURED IN THE UNITED STATES OF AMERICA

Contents

Introduction vii

January

January 4 Epiphany of the Lord 1
January 11 Baptism of the Lord 6
January 18 Second Sunday after the Epiphany 11
January 25 Third Sunday after the Epiphany 16

February

February 1 Fourth Sunday after the Epiphany 21
February 8 Fifth Sunday after the Epiphany 26
February 15 Transfiguration Sunday 31
February 18 Ash Wednesday 36
February 22 First Sunday in Lent 41

March

March 1 Second Sunday in Lent 45
March 8 Third Sunday in Lent 50
March 15 Fourth Sunday in Lent 54
March 22 Fifth Sunday in Lent 58
March 29 Palm/Passion Sunday 63

April

April 2 Holy Thursday 68
April 3 Good Friday 74
April 5 Easter Sunday 78

CONTENTS

April 12 Second Sunday of Easter 84
April 19 Third Sunday of Easter 89
April 26 Fourth Sunday of Easter 94

May

May 3 Fifth Sunday of Easter 99
May 10 Sixth Sunday of Easter 104
May 17 Ascension Sunday 109
May 24 Pentecost Sunday 114
May 31 Trinity Sunday 119

June

June 7 Second Sunday after Pentecost 123
June 14 Third Sunday after Pentecost 128
June 21 Fourth Sunday after Pentecost 133
June 28 Fifth Sunday after Pentecost 138

July

July 5 Sixth Sunday after Pentecost 142
July 12 Seventh Sunday after Pentecost 148
July 19 Eighth Sunday after Pentecost 152
July 26 Ninth Sunday after Pentecost 157

August

August 2 Tenth Sunday after Pentecost 162
August 9 Eleventh Sunday after Pentecost 167
August 16 Twelfth Sunday after Pentecost 173
August 23 Thirteenth Sunday after Pentecost 177
August 30 Fourteenth Sunday after Pentecost 182

CONTENTS

September

September 6 Fifteenth Sunday after Pentecost 188
September 13 Sixteenth Sunday after Pentecost 194
September 20 Seventeenth Sunday after Pentecost. . . . 199
September 27 Eighteenth Sunday after Pentecost. 203

October

October 4 Nineteenth Sunday after Pentecost. 207
October 11 Twentieth Sunday after Pentecost 212
October 18 Twenty-First Sunday after Pentecost 216
October 25 Twenty-Second Sunday after Pentecost . . . 220

November

November 1 Twenty-Third Sunday after Pentecost/
All Saints Sunday. 224
November 8 Twenty-Fourth Sunday after Pentecost . . 228
November 15 Twenty-Fifth Sunday after Pentecost . . . 232
November 22 Reign of Christ Sunday 237
November 26 Thanksgiving Day. 243
November 29 First Sunday of Advent 247

December

December 6 Second Sunday of Advent. 251
December 13 Third Sunday of Advent 255
December 20 Fourth Sunday of Advent 260
December 24 Christmas Eve. 266
December 27 First Sunday after Christmas 270

Contributors 275
Scripture Index. 279

Introduction to the Final Edition

Planning and leading worship is a unique calling that challenges the best of us. It seems like only yesterday when worship planners were praised for coordinating scripture with liturgy, preaching, and hymns. And if the choir anthem fit the theme, worship was considered amazing. Now, worship leaders are faced with demands for diverse music and worship styles, and eye-catching on-screen presentations. Add in multimedia, visuals, texting, posting on social media so worshipers will find and follow your church online, and the pressures placed upon worship planners can become overwhelming. To help you meet the demands of this awesome responsibility, we offer *The Abingdon Worship Annual 2026* as a resource and partner in your planning process.

In *The Abingdon Worship Annual 2026*, you will again find the words of many different authors, poets, pastors, laypersons, and theologians. Some authors have written for this resource before, others provide a fresh voice. Since the contributing authors represent a wide variety of denominational and theological backgrounds, their words will vary in style and content. Feel free to combine, edit, or adapt the words within these pages to fit the needs of your congregation and the style of your worship. (Notice the reprint permission for worship given on the copyright page of this book.) In these pages, we provide theme ideas and all the written and spoken elements of worship, following the Revised Common Lectionary. For the non-lectionary congregations, you'll find the scripture index particularly helpful in choosing prayers and readings that fit your context. Although the *Worship Annual* does not

INTRODUCTION

address the visual, video, musical, and emerging resources that many worship services require, you can find all of these materials in our *Creative Worship Made Easy*: https://www.creativeworshipmadeeasy.com.

Each entry provides suggestions that follow an order of service that may be adapted to address your specific worship practice and format. Feel free to re-order or pick and choose the various resources to fit the needs of your worship services and congregations. Each entry follows a thematic focus arising from one or more of the week's scriptures.

To fit the Basic Pattern of Christian Worship—reflecting a flow that leads from a time of gathering and praise into a time of receiving and responding to the Word before moving into a time of sending forth—each entry includes Centering Words, Call to Worship and Opening Prayer, Prayer of Yearning and Words of Assurance, Response to the Word, Offertory Prayer, and Benediction. Communion resources are sometimes also included, but you can find a full collection of communion resources in our book *Is It Communion Sunday Already: Communion Resources for All Seasons*, available from Amazon.

Using the Worship Resources

Centering Words and **Calls to Worship** focus worshipers and gather God's people together as they prepare to worship. Often called "Greetings" or "Gathering Words," these words may be read by one worship leader or responsively. Regardless of how they are printed in this resource, feel free to experiment in your services of worship. They may be read antiphonally (back and forth) between two readers or two groups within the congregation: right and left sides of the sanctuary, choir and musicians, etc.

Opening Prayers in this resource are varied in form but typically invoke God's presence into worship. Whether formal, informal, general, or specific, these prayers serve to attune our hearts and minds to God. Although many may be adapted for use in other parts of the worship service, we have grouped them into the category "Opening Prayers."

Prayers of Yearning and **Words of Assurance** lead the people of God to connect with God in our deepest needs and yearnings, assuring us of God's forgiveness and grace. Regardless of how they are printed, whether unison or responsively, Prayers of Yearning and Words of Assurance may be spoken by a single leader, read in unison, or led by a small group. Some prayers may even be used as Opening, Closing, or Responsive Prayers.

Litanies and **Responsive Readings** offer additional avenues of congregational participation in our services of worship. Think creatively as you decide how to use these Responsive Readings in your service of worship: in unison, by a worship leader alone, or in a call and response format. Feel free to change the title of these liturgies to suit your worship setting.

Benedictions, sometimes called "Blessings" or "Words of Dismissal," send the congregation forth to continue the work of worship. Some of these Benedictions work best in call and response format; others work best when delivered as a blessing by a single worship leader. As always, use the format best suited to your congregation.

Communion liturgies are sometimes provided as well, each written specifically to relate to the thematic and scriptural focus of the day. Some follow the pattern of the Great Thanksgiving; others are Invitations to Communion or Communion Prayers of Consecration for the celebration of the Eucharist.

Although you will find *The Abingdon Worship Annual 2026* an invaluable tool for planning worship, it is but one piece of the puzzle for worship preparation. For additional music suggestions, you will want to consult *Prepare! An Ecumenical Music and Worship Planner* or *The United Methodist Music and Worship Planner*. These resources contain lengthy listings of lectionary-related hymns, praise songs, vocal solos, and choral anthems. As a final complement to your worship planning

INTRODUCTION

process, Mary also pens *Creative Worship Made Easy* as part of her worship subscription service, including video and film clip suggestions, screen visuals, popular song ideas, hands-on participation suggestions, along with series ideas, suggested sermon titles, and sermon starters for each Sunday. Explore Mary's *Creative Worship Made Easy* with a free trial at https://www.creativeworshipmadeeasy.com.

As you begin your worship planning, we recommend that you read the scriptures for each day, then meditate on the **Theme Ideas** suggested in this resource. Review the many words for worship printed herein and listen for the words that speak to you. Trust God's guidance and enjoy a wonderful year of worship and praise! Thank you for your many years of preparing and leading worship collaboratively with this resource. We pray God's blessings on your churches and your ministries. As always, please reach out directly to us if we can be of service in supporting your ministry through our coaching, writing, mentoring, or consulting.

Mary Scifres and B. J. Beu, Editors
The Abingdon Worship Annual 2004–2026
beuscifres@gmail.com

Our Thank You Gift to You

To thank you for your many years of faithful worship leadership alongside us, we'd like to offer our ebook *The Art of Extravagant Welcome*. Visit https://maryscifres.simplero.com/welcomebook for your free copy.

Introducing
Call & Response: The Abingdon Guidebook for Worship and Preaching, Year A

Pastors, music directors, worship directors, liturgists, musicians, and many others have long relied on *The Abingdon Worship Annual* as valuable tool for worship planning. Mary Scifres, BJ Beu, and a gifted group of writers have provided this excellent resource year after year.

Beginning with Advent 2025, a new tool is available, one which we hope meets the emerging needs of people who plan and lead worship and preaching at churches of all types. The new tool is *Call & Response: The Abingdon Guidebook for Worship and Preaching*.

Call and Response is structured around the Christian calendar, with resources for Advent, Lent, Pentecost, and the other seasons and special days of the Christian year. The volume is organized in two main parts.

Part One reminds readers of the time-honored pattern of worship: Gathering, Proclaiming, Thanksgiving, and Sending. It details each phase of worship, concisely explaining the primary elements, such as the Call to Worship, Passing of the Peace, Affirmation of Faith, Prayers of the People, Baptism, Holy Communion, Invitation to Discipleship, and Benediction. Examples, including the full text, are provided for each. Part One guides readers to recall (or learn) the meaning and significance of this pattern of worship, and empowers them to plan and lead with confidence.

Part Two equips readers with a treasure trove of ready-to-use texts for worship. It provides original prayers, litanies, and liturgies for each phase of the service. The material is organized by liturgical season, with multiple texts for each phase of worship. So, for example, readers can choose from a wide selection of Gathering Prayers during Lent, using the best option for their congregation each week of the season. The texts are based on the lectionary, but can be used for thematic worship too.

Call & Response also includes prompts for sermon development based on both thematic and lectionary approaches. And throughout the book, readers will find sidebars with instructive material related to the meaning, history, and logistics of worship and preaching. This resource is ideal for longtime pastors and people who are new to Christian worship planning, alike.

Call & Response Features:

- Full texts of prayers, litanies, and other liturgy for each phase of worship
- Organized by liturgical season
- Sidebars addressing special cases like trauma, natural disaster, current events, and patriotic days
- Examples and prompts for both lectionary- and theme-based sermons
- Liturgies for baptism and holy communion
- Sidebars with instruction about the meaning, history, and logistics of worship
- A wide and varied pool of contributor voices
- Material from ancient and contemporary sources
- Suggestions for engaging all generations together in worship

This new resource provides material for worship and sermon planning beginning in Advent. Order (or pre-order) a copy at cokesbury.com.

January 4, 2026

Epiphany of the Lord

Mary Scifres
Copyright © Mary Scifres

COLOR
White

SCRIPTURE READINGS
Isaiah 60:1-6; Psalm 72:1-7, 10-14; Ephesians 3:1-12; Matthew 2:1-12

THEME IDEAS

It's so intriguing that the celebration at the end of the Christmas season is labeled, "Epiphany," as if this was the sudden realization, the first recognition, the dramatic revelation that this baby Jesus is the long-awaited King of God's people. Centuries and millennia later, most Christians take for granted that Christ the King arrives on Christmas morning. But today's scriptures proclaim in a more pointed way that this child Jesus isn't just a mysterious revelation heralded by angelic appearances and shepherd visitations. Kings from the East travel afar to proclaim this child to be king of the Jews, a ruler of nations, and perhaps even a ruler of all the world. The pairing of Isaiah's prophecy, echoed by Psalm 72 and Ephesians 3, reminds us this is a day of profound revelation. The story of Christmas is much more than just a lullaby. This is the beginning of a new way of viewing the world, for Christ the King has come for all the world.

INVITATION AND GATHERING

CENTERING WORDS *(Isaiah 60, Ephesians 3)*
Shining for all to see, Christ has come. Shining in our hearts, Christ still lives in wisdom, power, and love.

CALL TO WORSHIP *(Ephesians 3, Matthew 2)*
In this holy season of Christmas,
Christ comes to us again.
In this quiet after the harried days of December,
God invites us to pause and reflect.
Our journey has led us here.
The Spirit is with us now.
Let us bow down as sages of old,
and worship Christ our King.

OPENING PRAYER *(Isaiah 60, Psalm 72, Ephesians 3, Matthew 2, New Year)*
Christ of power and justice,
    help us embrace the power that comes from love,
        and guide us to seek the justice that love reveals.
Open our hearts and minds,
    that we may hear your wisdom
        in this time of worship.
Open our lives in the year ahead
    to the power and strength of your loving Spirit.
In your holy name, we pray. Amen.

PROCLAMATION AND RESPONSE

PRAYER OF YEARNING *(Isaiah 60, Psalm 72, Ephesians 3, Matthew 2, John 8:12)*
Light of the world, we yearn to walk in the light,
    but the shadows are all around and oh-so-familiar.
Pull us from the darkness of fear of gloom—
    familiar places where we hide from you,
        from ourselves, and from others.

Shine upon us with your grace,
>   and pull us forward with your love.
> For we yearn for the courage of sages of old
>   who left hearth and home to draw closer to you.
> Give us the passion to stand up for justice,
>   to share our gifts and talents generously,
>   and to offer our love unconditionally.
> For we long to build your realm upon this earth. Amen.

WORDS OF ASSURANCE (Isaiah 60)
> Arise! Shine! Christ the light has come,
>   and this light will guide us well.

PASSING THE PEACE OF CHRIST (Psalm 72)
> May peace prosper in our world and in this place. And may we foster the abundance of peace by sharing signs of peace and love with one another.

INTRODUCTION TO THE WORD (Ephesians 3, Matthew 2)
> Paul may have thought this was a secret plan. The sages may have had to keep their secrets from Herod. But Christ's message is no secret. Listen, for God is still speaking and the Spirit's wisdom is constantly being revealed.

RESPONSE TO THE WORD or CALL TO WORSHIP (Isaiah 60, Ephesians 3)
> Shine, Jesus, shine.
>   **Shine in our hearts with grace.**
> Shine, Jesus, shine.
>   **Shine in our lives with justice.**
> Shine, Jesus, shine.
>   **Shine on our world with love.**
> *(This litany can follow or lead into the song "Shine, Jesus, Shine.")*

THANKSGIVING AND COMMUNION

INVITATION TO THE OFFERING *(Matthew 2)*
As the kings brought their gifts, so now we are invited to share our gifts. Whether giving online, in the offering plate, through the mail, or with our lives, our gifts are another way we give Christ our worship and we give God the glory. May the Spirit flow through us and through our giving in this time of offering and in the year ahead.

OFFERING PRAYER *(Psalm 72, Matthew 2)*
Gracious God, bless these gifts,
>that they may be as impactful as the gold,
>>frankincense, and myrrh given to the Christ child
>>>by kings long ago.

May our treasures bring honor to your name
>and support justice in your world.

May our worship bring humility to our hearts,
>and may our time and talents bring love to life
>>in all that we say and in all that we do. Amen.

INVITATION TO COMMUNION *(Psalm 72, Matthew 2)*
Come to the table of grace.
All are welcome here.
Come to the table of love.
This is the feast of God's compassion for all.
Come to the table of joy.
Christ invites us to celebrate his presence.

SENDING FORTH

BENEDICTION *(Isaiah 60, Psalm 72)*
Arise, shine, as you go into the world!
We will shine as we go into the world!
Shine with love and justice.
We will shine for all the world.

JANUARY 4, 2026

Notes

January 11, 2026

Baptism of the Lord

Rebecca Gaudino

COLOR
White

SCRIPTURE READINGS
Isaiah 42:1-9; Psalm 29; Acts 10:34-43; Matthew 3:13-17

THEME IDEAS

John the Baptist asks Jesus an interesting question when Jesus appears at the Jordan to be baptized: "... and do you come to me?" (Matthew 3:14, NRSVue). John thinks Jesus should be baptizing the Baptizer! Scholars suggest that John is talking about Jesus' blamelessness here. But what if John's question is also about our role in Jesus' work, our part in his ministry of justice, peace, and forgiveness that we might find surprising? After all, Jesus seeks John's consent to, and participation in, this unexpected baptism: "'Let it be so now, for it is proper for us in this way to fulfill all righteousness.' Then [John] consented" (Matthew 3:15). And with this partnership what scholars see as a mini-Genesis scene unfolds: the Spirit-Dove of creation hovers over the baptismal waters to rest on Jesus as it will soon hover as flame over the heads of Jesus' followers. Isaiah talks of God's choosing a servant to accomplish amazing aims, but

JANUARY 11, 2026

what follows is much more than divine decree, for God upholds, delights in, takes by the hand, sends God's Spirit—and the world changes! In the end, Jesus comes to us, too, hoping for our consent to bold actions in bringing about God's vision for our world.

INVITATION AND GATHERING

CENTERING WORDS *(Isaiah 42)*
I am your servant, Creator of All. I am your chosen.
May you delight in me!

CALL TO WORSHIP *(Isaiah 42, Matthew 3)*
Voice 1	You who created the heavens and stretched them out above us,
Voice 2	*You who spread out the earth beneath our feet and summoned sprouts and shoots,*
All	**Breathe life into us, God Who Creates!**
Voice 1	You who came to the river,
Voice 2	*You who sought the Baptizer and the Jordan waters,*
All	**Welcome us to the waters of life, Jesus the Christ!**
Voice 1	You who soared through the heavens,
Voice 2	*You who hovered and rested upon Jesus,*
All	**Alight upon us today, Spirit of God, Heaven's Dove.**

OPENING PRAYER *(Isaiah 42, Matthew 3)*
You Who Call Us, we come before you
    in answer your call in our life.
You created the heavens and the earth
    and placed us here for life and hope.
We know your dream for a world
    that is righteous and just,
        a world you promise will come to pass.
Breathe your Spirit upon us again and again,
    and bring to life our passion for your bold vision.

Make us lights to those who sit in darkness!
In the name of Jesus, who descended into the waters
> of baptism to show us the way to righteousness,
>> and of the Soaring Spirit, who alights upon those
>> who arise from these life-giving waters.
Amen.

PROCLAMATION AND RESPONSE

PRAYER OF YEARNING *(Isaiah 42, Matthew 3)*
God of Holy Expectation,
> when we read about those who serve you,
>> like John, like Jesus, those whom you love
>> and delight in, we yearn to feel your delight
>>> in us as well.

Our voices can seem weak, our efforts in vain.
Sometimes we feel like dimly burning wicks,
> just about to go out.

Sometimes *we* are the ones sitting in darkness,
> even though you call us to help others
>> find their way out of the darkness.

Holy One, take us by the hand.
Strengthen us in our weakness,
> that your holy work may be accomplished
>> through us and that we may know your delight
>>> in the core of who we are. Amen.

WORDS OF ASSURANCE *(Isaiah 42)*
Isaiah assures us that our weakness and limitation
> do not stand in the way of God's plans for the world
> or God's pleasure in us.

We are God's beloved children, God's partners
> in the work of world-renewing.

We are God's chosen in whom the Creator delights.

PASSING THE PEACE OF CHRIST *(Matthew 3)*
Jesus is the first one who passed through the waters of Christian baptism, Our Eldest Sibling in the new family of

God, Womb of Life, through whom all find new life. Let us welcome everyone who joins us in our family time today.

INTRODUCTION TO THE WORD (Isaiah 42, Matthew 3)
The prophet Isaiah speaks of those who live in the coastlands awaiting God's wisdom. Matthew tells the account of many who gather at the Jordan River to hear John preach and experience the waters of forgiveness and new life. Let us listen to our ancient sacred texts, texts that continue to teach us today and call us to the waters of renewal.

RESPONSE TO THE WORD (Matthew 3)
May we follow Jesus into the waters of new life
   and know that the Spirit of God comes to us, too.
Praise be to God, River of Forgiveness and Life,
River of Justice flowing through us in hope
   and power for the world!
(One song that fits as a sung response is "There's a River of Life" by L. Casebolt. Sing the first verse and chorus.)

THANKSGIVING AND COMMUNION

INVITATION TO THE OFFERING (Isaiah 42)
Isaiah calls those who partner with God a light to the nations. We are to establish justice in the earth and bring those who sit in darkness into the light. What important world-shaping work! May we give of our lives and gifts for this work!

OFFERING PRAYER (Isaiah 42)
God of Bold Visions for our World,
   you love all peoples and nations,
      seeking a world where everyone flourishes
         in just and righteous lives.
Use us and our gifts for the newness
   you declare possible.
Make this newness spring forth in and through us.
Amen.

SENDING FORTH

BENEDICTION (Matthew 3)
A surprised John asked Jesus,
". . . and do you come to me?"
Jesus came to him with a surprising request.
**Jesus comes to each of us, inviting us to bold
and hopeful action.**
So when God calls, when Jesus arrives,
we will answer the call and step forward.
We will bring hope to those suffering injustice,
and light to those in darkness,
Through the power of the Spirit,
we go to live our lives to the fullest. Amen.

Notes

January 18, 2026

Second Sunday after the Epiphany

B. J. Beu
Copyright © B. J. Beu

COLOR
Green

SCRIPTURE READINGS
Isaiah 49:1-7; Psalm 40:1-11; 1 Corinthians 1:1-9; John 1:29-42

THEME IDEAS

With a resounding "Yes," today's scriptures answer the question, "Can one person make a difference?" Isaiah proclaims a message for all Israel to hear: They will be a light to the nations. The psalmist confesses that the Lord has "put a new song in my mouth, a song of praise for our God" (Psalm 40:3). Paul preaches that he was "called by God's will to be an apostle of Christ Jesus" (1 Corinthians 1:1). Andrew hears of Jesus from John the Baptist and says to his brother: "We have found the Messiah" (John 1:41). It is easy to see the impact of Isaiah, the psalmist and Paul, but what of Andrew? What difference did he make? Andrew brought his brother Simon to Jesus—a brother whom Jesus renames Peter, a brother whom Jesus calls the rock. If we follow God's call, we can all make a difference, if only by inviting others onto the journey with us.

INVITATION AND GATHERING

CENTERING WORDS *(Isaiah 49, Psalm 40, 1 Corinthians 1, John 1)*
> Even the smallest person can change the world. Even the least among us can be a light that banishes the darkness.

CALL TO WORSHIP *(Isaiah 49, Psalm 40)*
> Listen, O coastlands.
> > **Pay attention, people of God.**
>
> We are called to be a light to the nations.
> > **We are created to sing of God's salvation.**
>
> Shout praise for God's faithfulness.
> > **Rejoice in our many gifts.**
>
> Come! Let us worship.

~or~

CALL TO WORSHIP *(Isaiah 49, Psalm 40, John 1)*
> Can you hear God's call?
> > **Christ's voice is heard far and near.**
>
> Can you discern God's Word?
> > **Christ calls one and all.**
>
> God speaks of light and life.
> > **Christ loves the mighty and the small.**
>
> The Spirit breathes joy and compassion.
> > **We are called into fellowship together.**

OPENING PRAYER *(Isaiah 49, 1 Corinthians 1)*
> Holy One, may our spirits be polished arrows
> > in the quiver of your searching love.
>
> May our words ring true with shouts of praise.
> Use us, Gracious God, as instruments
> > of your mercy and compassion.
>
> Fashion us into vessels of your abiding Spirit,
> > that a world torn by brokenness and pain
> > > might touch your healing love
> > > > through our fellowship with you
> > > > and with one another. Amen.

JANUARY 18, 2026

PROCLAMATION AND RESPONSE

PRAYER OF YEARINING *(Isaiah 49, Psalm 40, 1 Corinthians 1, John 1)*
    Merciful God, when we succumb to despair
        and get lost in our fears of inadequacy,
            remind us who we are and whose we are.
    We long to feel worthy of your love
        and to rest secure in your call
            to be a light to the nations.
    Remind us, Loving Presence,
        to speak words of hope like Isaiah,
            and words of encouragement like Paul.
    When others ask us if we have found the Lamb of God,
        give us the courage and the faith to boldly proclaim:
    "Come and see!" Amen.

WORDS OF ASSURANCE *(Isaiah 49, Psalm 40, 1 Corinthians 1)*
    God polishes us as arrows in the quiver of holy love.
    Christ calls us and sanctifies us to be the saints of God.
    The Spirit fills us with light and leads us home.

PASSING THE PEACE OF CHRIST *(Psalm 40, John 1)*
    With songs of joy in our mouths and songs of praise for our God, let us great one another and share the peace of our Lord, Jesus Christ.

RESPONSE TO THE WORD *(Isaiah 49, Psalm 40, 1 Corinthians 1)*
    Listen, O coastlands.
    Pay attention, you people of God.
    God's love shines within.
    We will be a light to the nations.
    Look within your hearts.
    We will follow the law of God written there.
    Listen, O coastlands.
    Pay attention, you people of God.

God shines within.
Amen and amen.

THANKSGIVING AND COMMUNION

INVITATION TO THE OFFERING (Isaiah 49, Psalm 40)
What does God require of us, and with what shall we come before the Lord? It is not with sacrifice and burnt offerings, but with hearts filled with praise and lives bent on justice. With joy and thanksgiving for the tender mercies of our God, may today's offering be a sign of our commitment to bring God's justice and compassion to our world.

OFFERING PRAYER (Isaiah 49, John 1)
God of Grace and God of Glory,
>you bless us with water and the Spirit,
>>that we might know the fullness of life.

As we strive to be a light to the nations,
>may others be brought to the dawn of your glory.

Bless the gifts we bring before you now,
>that they might reach the very ends of the earth
>>and help those struggling to find the light. Amen.

SENDING FORTH

BENEDICTION (Isaiah 49, Psalm 40, 1 Corinthians 1)
Sing a new song as you leave this place.
We go in the love of the One who strengthens us.
Heed the call that stirs within you.
We go in service of our call to follow Christ.
Walk forth as saints of God.
We go in fellowship with the Holy Spirit.
Bring hope to the ends of the earth.
We go to be a light to the nations.

JANUARY 18, 2026

Notes

January 25, 2026

Third Sunday after the Epiphany

Amy B. Hunter

COLOR

Green

SCRIPTURE READINGS

Isaiah 9:1-4; Psalm 27:1, 4-9; 1 Corinthians 1:10-18; Matthew 4:12-23

THEME IDEAS

Jesus' call to his first disciples interrupts all they believe to be routine and predictable about their lives. More than that, Jesus' call comes as his response to the real dangers he faces, made explicit in the arrest of John the Baptist. An audacious hope runs through today's readings. To those who have experienced gloom and anguish, God is Light. To those who face challenges, God is Sanctuary. To those caught up in divisions and rivalries, God is Unity through the cross. Jesus invites all people to follow him in proclaiming the nearness and the goodness of God's hoped-for kingdom.

JANUARY 5, 2026

INVITATION AND GATHERING

CENTERING WORDS *(Psalm 27, Matthew 4)*
Today and every day, Jesus says, "Come! Follow me." Today and every day, let us answer, "You, Lord Jesus, are the one we seek."

CALL TO WORSHIP *(Isaiah 9, 1 Corinthians 1, Matthew 4)*
Friends of God, today Jesus calls to each of us: "Come! Follow me!"
The kingdom of heaven has come near.
Some say, "But we are walking in darkness."
In Christ, we have seen God's light.
The kingdom of heaven has come near.
Some say, "But divisions tear us apart."
In Christ we are united in mind and purpose.
The kingdom of heaven has come near.
Friends of God, today we gather to worship God and to follow Jesus.
The kingdom of heaven has come near.

OPENING PRAYER *(Isaiah 9, Psalm 27, 1 Corinthians 1, Matthew 4)*
Inviting God, help us to hear Jesus calling us
    and help us to follow him.
In Christ, your kingdom draws near to us,
    whether we are seeking it or not.
When we are caught up in our anguish,
    you shine a great light in our darkness.
When we face days full of trouble,
    you shelter us.
When we are at odds with others,
    quarreling and breaking apart into factions,
        you save us with the unity won by Christ
            through the cross and his resurrection.

Whether we face danger or are at ease in our routines—
> the kingdom of heaven draws near and Jesus says:
>> "Now is the time to follow me."

You hear us, God, when we cry out to you.
May we hear you this day when you cry out to us.
Amen.

PROCLAMATION AND RESPONSE

PRAYER OF YEARNING (Isaiah 9, 1 Corinthians 1, Matthew 4)

> Jesus, you come into our lives
>> as a light shining in our darkness,
>>> and you call us to follow you.
>
> We long to seek you.
> We long to follow you.
> Sometimes our losses and failures overwhelm us,
>> and we don't hear your call.
>
> Sometimes we are caught up in our disagreements
>> and our desires to prevail,
>>> and we don't hear your call.
>
> Sometimes we are so busy with our responsibilities
>> and our successes, comfortable in our routines,
>>> and we don't hear your call.
>
> Yet, we have seen your great light.
> We have heard your appeal to come together
>> in mind and purpose.
>
> May we, like Peter and Andrew, and James and John,
>> step away from our darkness and our conflicts
>>> and our devotion to our set ways.
>
> Help us to hear your call,
>> for your kingdom draws near. Amen.

WORDS OF ASSURANCE (Psalm 27, Matthew 4)

> People of God, Jesus is with us today,
>> offering us God's kingdom and healing.

God is our light and our salvation,
> everything we need to be fully alive.
We have nothing to fear.

PASSING THE PEACE OF CHRIST *(Matthew 4)*
> Jesus calls us to follow him, sharing with one another the good news that God has drawn near to us. Let us begin by greeting one another with the peace of Jesus Christ.

INTRODUCTION TO THE WORD *(Psalm 27, Matthew 4)*
> Hear the word which calls us to follow Jesus Christ.
> **"Come!" our hearts say, "Let us seek God."**

RESPONSE TO THE WORD *(Psalm 27, Matthew 4)*
> This is the word about Jesus, the one who says, "Follow me."
> **Like the first disciples, let us turn from our distractions and follow Christ.**

THANKSGIVING AND COMMUNION

INVITATION TO THE OFFERING *(Isaiah 9, Psalm 27, 1 Corinthians 1, Matthew 4)*
> God has come to us as light, shelter, and unity, reminding us that the kingdom of heaven is very near to us. Let us respond immediately, offering ourselves and our gifts as signs of our joy.

OFFERING PRAYER *(Isaiah 9, 1 Corinthians 1, Matthew 4)*
> Generous God, you have blessed us with your call
>> to follow Jesus.
> In return, we rejoice as we give our offerings and gifts.
> May they be used for the work
>> of proclaiming the good news
>>> that the kingdom of heaven come near. Amen.

SENDING FORTH

BENEDICTION *(Isaiah 9, Psalm 27, 1 Corinthians 1, Matthew 4)*
May we leave worship today eager to follow Jesus.
To those in darkness, let us proclaim:
God is our light and our salvation.
To those in danger, let us proclaim:
God is our protection and shelter.
To those caught in conflicts and divisions,
let us proclaim:
Jesus Christ draws us together in mind and purpose.
Following Jesus, may we know and share the message:
The kingdom of heaven has come near.

Notes

February 1, 2026

Fourth Sunday after the Epiphany

B. J. Beu
Copyright © B. J. Beu

COLOR

Green

SCRIPTURE READINGS

Micah 6:1-8; Psalm 15; 1 Corinthians 1:18-31; Matthew 5:1-12

THEME IDEAS

God values humility, gentleness, justice, and mercy above displays of personal piety and striving for social approval. The wisdom of the world and the power and strength of personal success are to be scorned in favor of the blessings that come from humility, peacemaking, and righteous living. Those who seek to walk in righteousness are called to do justice, love kindness, and walk humbly with their God.

INVITATION AND GATHERING

CENTERING WORDS (*Micah 6, Psalm 15, 1 Corinthians 1, Matthew 5*)
Those who walk blamelessly, speak truthfully, and live gently are able to kneel before the Lord and not be put to shame must.

CALL TO WORSHIP *(Micah 6, Psalm 15, 1 Corinthians 1, Matthew 5)*
What does the Lord require of us?
To do justice, love kindness,
and walk humbly with our God.
With what shall we come before the Lord?
With speech that is gentle,
and words that build up.
How shall we live our faith?
With actions that bring peace,
and works that lift up the lowly.
Come and worship God in spirit and in truth.

OPENING PRAYER *(Micah 6, Psalm 15, 1 Corinthians 1)*
The hills hear your voice, O Lord.
The mountains quake before you.
As we call on your name,
help us walk in the ways of righteousness
and speak in tones of peace.
As we seek to be blameless and do what is right,
may our hearts be free from guile and deceit,
that we be known as peace makers,
the blessed children of God. Amen.

PROCLAMATION AND RESPONSE

PRAYER OF YEARINING *(Micah 6, Psalm 15, 1 Corinthians 1, Matthew 5)*
When we feel beaten down by the world, Merciful One,
free us from sorrow and grief.
When we are wounded by careless words,
help us refrain from lashing out in our suffering
and hurting the ones we love.
Fill us with a hunger and a thirst for righteousness,
that we may walk humbly in your ways
and be a blessing to everyone we meet. Amen.

WORDS OF ASSURANCE *(Micah 6, Matthew 5)*
God is stronger than our weaknesses,
  and greater than our failings.
Even when we fall short,
  God's love embraces us
  and sets us on the path of life once more.

PASSING THE PEACE OF CHRIST *(Matthew 5)*
Blessed are the peacemakers, for they shall be called children of God. As God's beloved children, let us share the peace that Christ brings with those around us.

RESPONSE TO THE WORD *(Micah 6, Matthew 5)*
Who does the will or the Lord?
  Those who bring justice, love kindness,
  and walk humbly with their God.
To whom does the kingdom of heaven belong?
  Those who are lowly and poor in spirit.
Who shall inherit the earth?
  Those who are meek and walk blamelessly
  before the Lord.
Who will be filled with good things?
  Those who hunger and thirst for righteousness.
Who shall see God?
  Those who are pure in heart.
Who shall be called children of God?
  Those are bring peace to our world.
Truly, these are blessed by the Lord, our God!

THANKSGIVING AND COMMUNION

INVITATION TO THE OFFERING *(Micah 6:6-8 NRSVUE)*
"With what shall I come before the Lord
  and bow myself before God on high?
Shall I come before him with burnt offerings,
  with calves a year old?
Will the Lord be pleased with thousands of rams,

with ten thousands of rivers of oil?
Shall I give my firstborn for my transgression,
    the fruit of my body for the sin of my soul?"
He has told you, O mortal, what is good,
    and what does the Lord require of you
but to do justice and to love kindness
    and to walk humbly with your God?"
In this spirit, let us bring our offerings before the Lord.

OFFERING PRAYER *(Micah 6, Matthew 5)*
Source of justice and mercy,
    work through this offering
        to bring your gifts to the world:
            righteousness and peace,
                love and kindness, hope and joy.
May our gifts truly express our gratitude
    for your many blessings for our church
        and for your children everywhere. Amen.

SENDING FORTH

BENEDICTION (Micah 6, Psalm 15, Matthew 5)
Seek justice and discover God's blessings.
    We will walk humbly with our God.
Practice kindness and touch Christ's presence.
    We will live in Christ's Way of peace.
Share mercy and abide in the Holy Spirit.
    **We will leave footprints of light and compassion
    with every step we take.**

FEBRUARY 1, 2026

Notes

February 8, 2026

Fifth Sunday after the Epiphany

Karin Ellis

COLOR
Green

SCRIPTURE READINGS
Isaiah 58:1-9a (9b-12); Psalm 112:1-9 (10);
1 Corinthians 2:1-12 (13-16); Matthew 5:13-20

THEME IDEAS

As we continue our journey through the season of Epiphany, today's lessons remind us to shine the light we have been given by God. Isaiah calls to the people and reminds them that what God really desires is for them to take care of each other, to bring about justice and healing. The psalmist echoes this thought, proclaiming that those who are righteous will be remembered. Paul reminds the Corinthians that he has proclaimed not only a message about the crucified and risen Christ, but also that the Spirit has given them gifts to use. And Matthew continues this theme with his proclamation to "let your light shine." The season of Epiphany may be drawing to a close, but the scriptures implore us to keep allowing the light of God to shine through us in all we do.

FEBRUARY 8, 2026

INVITATION AND GATHERING

CENTERING WORDS *(Isaiah 58, Matthew 5)*
In the beginning God brought forth light out of the darkness. This light has shown throughout the centuries in the lives of prophets and teachers, young and old, and in the life of Christ. This light still shines today in you. Let your light shine!

CALL TO WORSHIP *(Psalm 112)*
Praise the Lord!
Happy are those who delight in the Lord!
We come to this place, where generations before us have gathered.
Here we remember the light of God that shines in our lives.
Here we allow God's light to shine through us.
Let us worship our radiant God.
Praise the Lord!
Happy are we who delight in the Lord!

OPENING PRAYER *(Isaiah 58, 1 Corinthians 2)*
Amazing God, you have gathered us from many places
    to come together and praise you this day.
For this we are grateful!
As we worship today,
    may our minds be opened to learn your wisdom.
May our eyes be opened to places that need healing.
May our hands be opened to do your good work.
May our hearts be opened to your Holy Spirit,
    who gifts us and guides us.
In the name of Christ, we pray. Amen.

PROCLAMATION AND RESPONSE

PRAYER OF CONFESSION (Isaiah 58, Matthew 5)
There are times in our lives when we mess up, when we turn away from God, whether intentionally or unintentionally. There are times when we ignore God's presence in our lives or blatantly speak against God. It is because of these moments that we need to come before God to confess and receive forgiveness, knowing that God's grace is abundant. So, let us pray:

Merciful God, forgive us when we ignore you
    or your lessons for our lives.
Forgive us for allowing oppression and discord
    to flourish.
Forgive us for not feeding those who are hungry.
Forgive us for not providing shelter
    to those who have no place to lay down at night.
Forgive us for not repairing the broken places
    in our community.
O Lord, forgive us and then help us
    do your work of bringing about justice and healing.
Shine your light through us,
    so that all may come to know your abundant love.
Amen.

WORDS OF ASSURANCE (Isaiah 58)
When we call out to God, God is there to hear us.
Know that your prayers have been heard.
Now, receive the grace of God
    and live in God's abundant mercy.

FEBRUARY 8, 2026

PASSING THE PEACE OF CHRIST *(1 Corinthians 2)*
Generations before us have shared the peace of Christ with the faithful. Today we are here to continue the tradition as we share the peace of Christ with one another. Together, with God's Spirit, let us share the peace of Christ:

May the peace of Christ be with you.
And also with you!

PRAYER OF PREPARATION *(1 Corinthians 2)*
Holy One, search us and reveal your truths to us.
May your Spirit help us truly comprehend
    your message for us today. Amen.

RESPONSE TO THE WORD *(Matthew 5)*
Jesus promises that those who do the will of God will be called great in the kingdom of heaven.
May the words we have heard today inspire us to keep doing God's good work so that all of our lights will shine brightly. Amen.

THANKSGIVING

INVITATION TO THE OFFERING *(Psalm 112)*
We are told that giving freely to help others glorifies God. Let us bring our gifts to God, so that God's love may be made known.

OFFERING PRAYER *(Isaiah 58)*
Abundant God, we are grateful for the ways
    you bless our lives and for the gifts you give us.
May these gifts help heal and restore our community,
    so that all will flourish like a well-watered garden.
Amen.

SENDING FORTH

BENEDICTION (Isaiah 58, 1 Corinthians 2, Matthew 5)
May the love of God bring forth healing and restoration
  all of your days.
May the light of Christ guide your way.
And may the Holy Spirit empower you
  to do the good work of God. Amen.

Notes

February 15, 2026

Transfiguration Sunday

B. J. Beu
Copyright © B. J. Beu

COLOR
White

SCRIPTURE READINGS
Exodus 24:12-18; Psalm 99; 2 Peter 1:16-21; Matthew 17:1-9

THEME IDEAS
God tells Moses to go up the mountain and wait—wait for instruction, wait for a taste of God's awesome power, wait for the next big experience of the holy. As people of faith, we spend a lot of time waiting. Yet, it seems that we are never quite ready when the moment of revelation and mystery arrives. Transfiguration Sunday is about God's light and power; but it is also about waiting and being ready when God's light shines upon us.

INVITATION AND GATHERING

CENTERING WORDS *(Exodus 24, Matthew 17)*
Glory fills the skies, as we see Christ transformed before our very eyes.

CALL TO WORSHIP (Exodus 24, Matthew 17)

Climb the mountain of God.
We will watch and wait.
Wait for God's glory to shine like the sun.
Wait for Christ to reveal the heart of God.
Wait to gain courage for the terror of the night.
Wait for the Spirit to dispel the darkness.
Climb the mountain of God.
We will watch for things worth waiting for.

~or~

CALL TO WORSHIP (Psalm 99)

Come worship the Lord.
Praise the Lord on high.
Worship the Lord from the mountaintop.
Worship our Lord and King.
Let the earth quake and the people tremble.
Let the nations revere the Lord of life.

OPENING PRAYER (Exodus 24, Matthew 17)

Source of light and love, reveal to us your glory.
As you appeared to your servant Moses
 in devouring fire on Mount Sinai,
  appear to us now in power and might
   during our time of worship.
As you revealed Christ's resplendent light
 to his disciples on the mountaintop,
  reveal your radiant light to us
   during our fellowship together.
Transform us with your glory,
 that our souls might shine your light
  into a world shrouded in darkness. Amen.

FEBRUARY 15, 2026

PROCLAMATION AND RESPONSE

PRAYER OF YEARNING *(Exodus 24, Matthew 17)*
   Mighty God, we yearn to be called on a journey
      to climb your mountain of love and light.
   We long for the courage of Moses
      as we wait for your appearance,
         even when your powerful presence
            is like a devouring fire.
   Test our hearts, O God,
      that we might face our fears
         and prove ourselves worthy
            of your holy calling. Amen.

WORDS OF ASSURANCE *(Matthew 17)*
   With tenderness and grace, Jesus shows us the power
      and the glory of God.
   Walk in the assurance of God's mercy
      and the promise of Christ's strength for the journey.

PASSING THE PEACE OF CHRIST *(Exodus 24, Matthew 17)*
   As we climb the mountain of God to see Jesus transfigured in our midst, bless those on the journey with us with signs of Christ's peace.

INTRODUCTION TO THE WORD *(2 Peter 1)*
   The word of God is a lamp shining in the darkness, bringing hope until the day dawns and the morning star rises in our hearts. Listen for the word of God.

RESPONSE TO THE WORD *(Exodus 24, Psalm 99, 2 Peter 1, Matthew 17)*
   God speaks from the mountains above.
   God speaks from the earth below.
   God speaks that we might hear.
   God speaks that we might know.
   God speaks in promises of the past
      and in assurances of hope for the future.
   Thanks be to God.

THANKSGIVING AND COMMUNION

OFFERING PRAYER
>Light of Light, even when our dreams grow dark,
>>you bless us with your radiance and your love.
>
>Illumine the gifts we bring before you now,
>>that the world may see your light
>>>in the shadows of our world.
>
>Illumine our very lives,
>>that our souls may shine with Christ
>>>and bring his hope wherever we go. Amen.

SENDING FORTH

BENEDICTION (*Exodus 24, 2 Peter 1, Matthew 17*)
>Climb the mountain of God.
>>**We will walk in the light and truth of God.**
>
>Do not fear the voice that calls from the heavens.
>>**We will heed our call to follow Jesus.**
>
>Draw near to God's holy fire.
>>**We will bathe in the warmth of our God.**
>
>Shine the light of Christ in the world.
>>**We will be bold, for God goes with us.**

Notes

February 18, 2026

Ash Wednesday

Leigh Anne Taylor

COLOR
Purple

SCRIPTURE READINGS
Joel 2:1-2, 12-17; Psalm 51:1-17; 2 Corinthians 5:20b–6:10; Matthew 6:1-6, 16-21

THEME IDEAS
The song of the Ash Wednesday lectionary readings begins with a fanfare from Joel's trumpet announcing that the day of the Lord is near. In verse one, Joel calls for every person to return to God in true repentance—with weeping, fasting, and broken hearts. David's psalm sings the second verse, a perfect example of an honest confession and plea to God for restoration. Paul's third verse pleas for the Corinthians to be reconciled with God. Jesus' teaching in the Gospel of Matthew brings the song home with his instruction to pray, fast, and give in secret, where God alone can see.

FEBRUARY 18, 2026

INVITATION AND GATHERING

CENTERING WORDS *(Joel 2)*
How do you hear the phrase, "Repent and return to the Lord"? Do you hear tones of accusation, judgement, shaming? Or do you hear a loving invitation, resounding with compassion and warmth, with gentle guidance and welcome to our long-lost God-home?

CALL TO WORSHIP *(Joel 2)*
Repent and return to the Lord!
Repent? Wait... what did I do?
Repent and return to the Lord!
Return? Wait... where did I go?
Repent and return to the Lord!
Lord? Wait... is that you?
Beloved, I am calling you home to me.
Lord, I am on my way.

OPENING PRAYER *(Joel 2)*
Loving God, we gather for worship
   on this Ash Wednesday
      to examine the direction of our lives.
(pause for reflection)
We gather to notice where we are off course
   from our eternal destination.
(pause for reflection)
We gather to turn our faces back home, toward you.
(pause for reflection)
We gather to return to a loving relationship with you,
   with ourselves, and with one another.
(pause for reflection)
Thank you God for calling us home.
We love you, Lord. Amen.

PROCLAMATION AND RESPONSE

PRAYER OF YEARNING (Psalm 51, Matthew 6)
    Gracious God, as the forty days of Lent begin,
        it may take us forty days to admit everything
            that keeps us from fully living
                your divine love and compassion.
    Merciful God, we may need forty whole days
        to see and name and release
            our practiced patterns of denial.
    Compassionate God, it may take us forty days
        to hear and name and release
            the well-rehearsed scripts in our heads—
                scripts that defend us against our unloving
                    thoughts, words, and actions.
    Forgiving God, we are afraid that if we don't
        see and name and release our denial and defenses,
            the fearful and broken parts of us
                will remain unhealed
                    by your whole-making love.
    We don't want to live like that anymore.
    So Loving God, we open ourselves
        to your transforming love these forty days of Lent.
    Be with us as we weep for every part of ourselves
    that is fearful and broken.
        Help us see and name and release everything
            that would separate us from your love.
    Show us how to receive and give love
        as generously as you do.
    May your healing, loving life become our living prayer,
        as we become one with you and with one another.
    Amen.

WORDS OF ASSURANCE (2 Corinthians 5)
Right now—this is the acceptable time.
Today—this is the day of healing and restoration.
No obstacle stands in the way of God's love.
We are reconciled with God!
Thanks be to God!
Amen!

PRAYER OF PREPARATION (Psalm 51)
God of our healing and whole-making,
you desire truth in the inward being.
So let your truth, proclaimed in scripture,
song, and sermon, teach us wisdom
in our secret hearts.
Amen.

RESPONSE TO THE WORD (Psalm 51)
By the power of your holy word,
create in us a clean heart, O God,
and renew a right spirit within us.
Amen.

THANKSGIVING AND COMMUNION

OFFERING PRAYER (Psalm 51)
O Lord, open our lips,
and our mouths will declare your praise.
You created everything good,
and everything we have is from you.
Receive these gifts that we gratefully offer.
These are the fruits of our labor.
Receive also our lives, Loving God.
In everything, we would honor you. Amen.

SENDING FORTH

BENEDICTION (Psalm 51, Matthew 6)
  Beloved of God, as we open yourselves to God's
  transforming love for these forty days of Lent,
    **God will be with us as we weep for every part
    of ourselves that is fearful and broken.**
  God will help us see, name, and release
  everything that would separate us from God's love.
    **God will show us how to receive and give love
    as generously as God does.**
  Now receive this blessing:
  May your healing, loving life become a living prayer.
    We will become one with God.
  Go in peace.
    Amen.

Notes

February 22, 2026

First Sunday in Lent

Karen Clark Ristine

COLOR
Purple

SCRIPTURE READINGS
Genesis 2:15-17; 3:1-7; Psalm 32; Romans 5:12-19; Matthew 4:1-11

THEME IDEAS
As we enter the season of Lent, we set our intentions on the journey. In this season of self-examination and reflection, we trust the promise of God's steadfast love and infinite wisdom. We follow the ministry and examples of Christ. We attune ourselves to the guiding and caring presence of the Holy Spirit. Temptations and trials are part of any life; our faith allows us to examine our short-comings, embrace grace, and thrive.

INVITATION AND GATHERING

CENTERING WORDS (Psalm 32:11, NRSV)
"Be glad in the Lord and rejoice, O righteous, and shout for joy, all you upright in heart."

CALL TO WORSHIP *(Genesis 3, Psalm 32, Romans 5)*
Be glad in the Lord and rejoice.
> **Steadfast love surrounds those who trust the Lord.**

When we confess our transgressions,
Christ's grace and forgiveness encompass us.
> **Steadfast love surrounds those who trust the Lord.**

Open yourselves to the teachings and wisdom of the Spirit.
> **Steadfast love surrounds those who trust the Lord.**

OPENING PRAYER *(Psalm 32, Romans 5, Matthew 4)*
Gracious and Loving God, we seek the freedom
> found in the grace we receive through Christ Jesus.

We seek to know more fully your great love.
Turn us from our temptations.
Inspire us to open ourselves to the way of Christ,
> that as we examine our lives and live out these days,
>> we may become examples of your abundant love for all people.

May your Divine Spirit tend us
> as angels attended Jesus in the wilderness,
>> and may we feel revived and sustained to follow Jesus. Amen.

PROCLAMATION AND RESPONSE

PRAYER OF CONFESSION *(Matthew 4)*
Just as Jesus faced temptations in the wilderness,
> we too struggle with desires for power, glory, or riches.

Teach us to turn from these temptations
> and to turn toward the power of scripture and prayer.

Center us in our faith.
Lead us not into temptation,
>but deliver us from evil. Amen.

WORDS OF ASSURANCE *(Psalm 32)*
Many are the torments of the wicked, but steadfast love
>surrounds those who trust the Lord.
Be glad in the Lord and rejoice, O righteous,
>and shout for joy, all you upright in heart.

PASSING THE PEACE OF CHRIST *(Psalm 32, Romans 5, Matthew 4)*
May the grace, the steadfast love, and the peace
of Christ be with you all.
>**And also with you.**
Please offer one another a sign of Christ's love
and peace.

RESPONSE TO THE WORD
We seek to follow you, dear Jesus,
through the wildernesses of our lives.
Help us to see and turn from our own temptations,
that we might offer all glory and power to you.

THANKSGIVING AND COMMUNION

OFFERING PRAYER *(Psalm 32, Matthew 4)*
We offer ourselves to you, Lord Jesus,
>emptying ourselves to become your vessels
>>of love and grace and hope to all we encounter.
May the gift of our lives and the gifts of our service
>create God's kingdom on earth,
>>as it is in heaven. Amen.

THE ABINGDON WORSHIP ANNUAL 2026

SENDING FORTH

BENEDICTION
And so now go—
knowing that God's steadfast love surrounds you, knowing that Christ leads through your temptations,
knowing that the Holy Spirit tends you with care.
Go in peace.
Stay in Courage. Amen.

Notes

March 1, 2026

Second Sunday in Lent

B. J. Beu
Copyright © B. J. Beu

COLOR

Purple

SCRIPTURE READINGS

Genesis 12:1-4a; Psalm 121; Romans 4:1-5, 13-17; John 3:1-17

THEME IDEAS

The readings from Genesis and the Gospel of John speak of God's blessings. God blesses us that we, in return, might be a blessing to others. If Abram will set out in faith, God promises to bless those who bless him, and curse those who curse him. And John assures us that God's Son was not sent into the world to condemn the world, but to save it. How can our response to God be anything less than extending such blessing to others? Psalm 121 makes it clear that the one who helps us and keeps us from evil is the same God who created the heavens and the earth.

INVITATION AND GATHERING

CENTERING WORDS (Genesis 12)
God calls us and blesses us, that we might share our blessings with others.

CALL TO WORSHIP OR BENEDICTION (Genesis 12, Psalm 121)
God calls us to set out in faith.
The love of God leads us home.
Christ blesses us that we might bless others.
The blessings of Christ heal our world.
The Holy Spirit strengthens us for the journey.
The power of the Spirit sustains and supports us.
The One who made heaven and earth meets us here.

OPENING PRAYER (John 3)
Lord of light and love, your Spirit enlivens our spirits,
    even as your kingdom draws us to you.
May we be born from above,
    that our souls might ascend to your realm
        and taste the joy of eternal life in your name.
For you sent your Son into our world,
    not to condemn the world,
        but that all who enter into his light
            we might have life,
                and have it abundantly. Amen.

PROCLAMATION AND RESPONSE

PRAYER OF YEARNING (Genesis 12, Psalm 121, John 3)
Maker of heaven and earth, when we face times of trial,
lift our eyes to the hills to find our help.

For you meet us in our need,
  and you lift us from the cares and toils
    that weaken our spirits and sap our strength.
Call us this day as you called your followers of old,
  for we long experience your awesome power
    and respond with faithful hearts
      and willing spirits.
Bless us each day,
  that we might share the promise of your blessings
    with a world struggling to find its way. Amen.

WORDS OF ASSURANCE (John 3)
Just as the wind blows where it will,
  God's Spirit moves in our world,
    calling us into ever deeper life with Christ.
Hear and claim this good news.
It is freely given.

PASSING THE PEACE OF CHRIST (John 3)
As disciples of Christ, we are born of the Spirit and offered a heritage that no one can take away. Share the joy and peace of life in Christ by greeting those around you in the name of the one who came to save us in holy love.

RESPONSE TO THE WORD (John 3, Genesis 12)
Living Spirit, you move within us
  like an ever-flowing stream.
Your blessings blow through our world
  like the wind through the prairie.
You grace a weary world with newness of life
  and vitality of spirit.
Reside in our hearts and nourish our souls,
  that we might be born from above
    and abide in your grace. Amen.

CALL TO PRAYER (Psalm121, John 3)
The One who made heaven and earth is listening.
The One who renews our spirits and keeps us from evil
  is with us to hear our prayers.

The One who came, not to condemn the world
  but to save it, invites us to lift our eyes to the hills
  and seek the One who is our help.
(A time for silent prayer or Prayers of the People may follow.)

THANKSGIVING AND COMMUNION

OFFERING PRAYER *(Genesis 12, John 3)*
Gracious God, just as you blessed the saints of old
  when they ventured forth in faith,
    so now bless us in our living and in our giving.
Transform our gifts and offerings
  into blessings for a weak and weary world,
    that all may touch your great love. Amen.

SENDING FORTH

BENEDICTION *(John 3)*
Feel the Spirit blow through your life,
  renewing your spirit and calling you
    to be born from above.
Go in the love of God, the peace of Christ,
  and the strength of the Holy Spirit.

~or~

BENEDICTION *(Psalm 121:5-6, 8 NRSVUE)*
Hear the words of the psalmist.
  "The Lord is your keeper.
  The Lord is your shade at your right hand.
  The sun shall not strike you by day,
    nor the moon by night.
  The Lord will keep your going out
    and your coming in
      from this time on and forevermore."
Go with the blessings of God.

MARCH 1, 2026

Notes

March 8, 2026

Third Sunday in Lent

B. J. Beu
Copyright © B. J. Beu

COLOR

Purple

SCRIPTURE READINGS

Exodus 17:1-7; Psalm 95; Romans 5:1-11; John 4:5-42

THEME IDEAS

Without water to drink, the people perish. Without the waters of faith, our spirits wither and die. God offers us both, and therein lies our good news and our hope. In Exodus, the Hebrews cried out to God and received water from a rock. In John, a woman at the well met Jesus and was offered waters that well up to eternal life. The psalmist entreats us to give thanks to the One who is the source of our hope and salvation. And Romans reminds us that God's love has been poured into our hearts through the power of the Holy Spirit. These scriptures remind us just who it is that quenches our thirst.

MARCH 8, 2026

INVITATION AND GATHERING

CENTERING WORDS *(Exodus17, Romans 5, John 4)*
Water gushes from a rock. Living waters well up to eternal life. Come and drink deeply. Taste and see that our God is good.

CALL TO WORSHIP *(Psalm 95)*
Worship God with joy and thanksgiving.
Make a joyful noise to the rock of our salvation.
We are the sheep of God's pasture.
We are the lambs of God's flock.
Come! Let us worship the Lord.

OPENING PRAYER *(Exodus17, Romans 5, John 4)*
Living water, flow through our hearts today.
Quench our thirst in our desert wanderings,
  and strengthen us for the road ahead.
Bathe us in your fountain of eternal life,
  that our spirits may flow with faith and love,
    through the power of your eternal Spirit. Amen.

PROCLAMATION AND RESPONSE

PRAYER OF YEARNING *(Exodus 17)*
Wellspring of salvation, quench our thirst this day.
When our souls are parched,
  we long to taste the healing waters
    of your grace.
When our spirits are as dry as desert sands,
  we yearn to find renewal in the well
    of your mercy and your love.
Shower us in your living water
  that we may be washed clean in the river
    of your forgiveness and your grace. Amen.

WORDS OF ASSURANCE (John 4)
>Those whose souls drink of Christ's living water
>>will never thirst again.
>Those who refresh themselves in Christ
>>will have a spring of water
>>welling up to eternal life.

PASSING THE PEACE OF CHRIST (Romans 5)
>God pours peace and love into our hearts through the power of the Holy Spirit. Let us receive these gifts, as we share the peace of Christ with one another.

INTRODUCTION TO THE WORD (Exodus 17, John 4)
>Listen, all who are thirsty!
>>**God bathes us in the waters of life.**
>Take heed, all who are weary and heavy laden.
>>**Christ offers us living waters to drink.**
>Pay attention, all who need the healing of God's Spirit.
>>**The Spirit renews our lives.**
>Listen for the word of God.

RESPONSE TO THE WORD (Romans 5, John 4)
>Spring of eternal life, well up within us.
>Wash away our fears and sweep aside the hurdles
>>that keep our hearts from embracing life
>>>and from renewing our spirits in your grace.
>Give us the confidence to share the good news
>>of your mercy and compassion
>>>with everyone we meet.
>In the promise of your grace, we pray. Amen.

THANKSGIVING AND COMMUNION

INVITATION TO OFFERING (Romans 5, John 4)
>Called to live in hope; invited to abide in joy, let us share the blessings we have so richly received from God.

MARCH 8, 2026

OFFERING PRAYER (Exodus17, John 4)
  Eternal Spirit, Source of healing and wholeness,
    receive our grateful hearts for your many blessings.
  Transform the gifts we bring this day
    into Christ's promise of living water
      for the world.
  Bathe those who are touched by today's offering
    in your goodness and grace,
      through Jesus Christ, our Lord. Amen.

SENDING FORTH

BENEDICTION (Exodus17, Romans 5, John 4)
  Bathe in the river of God's love.
  Swim in the waters of Christ's baptism.
  Ride the ocean currents of the Holy Spirit.
  Be renewed in the warm springs of our God.

Notes

March 15, 2026

Fourth Sunday in Lent

Mary Scifres
Copyright © Mary Scifres

COLOR
Purple

SCRIPTURE READINGS
1 Samuel 16:1-13; Psalm 23; Ephesians 5:8-14; John 9:1-41

THEME IDEAS
Our human way of seeing falls short without some God-corrected eyes to help us see rightly. All of today's scriptures invite us to see the world a bit differently than our human eyes and our human experience might perceive at first glance. By looking more deeply, with the inspiration of God, we are invited to see beyond appearances and beyond the world's expectations to the miraculous guidance and vision of God.

INVITATION AND GATHERING

CENTERING WORDS (1 Samuel 16, John 9)
Open the eyes of my heart, O God. Help us see more clearly, think more openly, feel more deeply, and love more abundantly.

MARCH 15, 2026

CALL TO WORSHIP (Ephesians 5, John 9, 1 Samuel 16, Psalm 23)
    Come into the light of God.
        Christ's brightness will guide our way.
    Come into the wisdom of God.
        The Spirit's insight will reveal new truths.
    Come into the praise of God,
        Worship opens new doors in our hearts.

OPENING PRAYER (1 Samuel 16, Psalm 23, Ephesians 5, John 9)
    Shepherd of love, guide our steps,
        open the eyes of our hearts,
            and fling wide the doors of our minds
                to perceive as you perceive.
    Open our lives to love as you love.
    Open our world to become the world you envision
        for your creation.
    In the light of your love, we pray. Amen.

PROCLAMATION AND RESPONSE

PRAYER OF YEARNING (John 9, 1 Samuel 16, Psalm 23, Ephesians 5)
    Christ our Healer, we want to see and be seen fully.
    We long to heal and be healed fully.
    We yearn to love and be loved fully.
    Yet, these desires seem beyond our reach
        when our minds are set on earthly things.
    Set our minds instead on you.
    Help us perceive the possibilities of fullness,
        of shalom, of your realm on this earth.
    Then guide us to help live into the reality
        you show us. Amen.

WORDS OF ASSURANCE *(Psalm 23, Ephesians 5)*
    Surely goodness and faithful love follow us
        all the days of our lives.
    For these gifts are already ours through the grace
        and the power of Christ Jesus.

PASSING THE PEACE OF CHRIST *(Ephesians 5)*
    As Christ's light has guided us here, may Christ's light shine in and through us that we may love and guide one another. Let's share signs of light with one another as we pass the peace of Christ.

RESPONSE TO THE WORD *(Ephesians 5, John 9, 1 Samuel 16)*
    Once lost in darkness,
        we now live in the light.
    Once blinded by earthly perceptions,
        we now see with the eyes of Christ's love.
    Once limited by human perceptions,
        **we now embrace the power of God's Spirit
        to bring God's realm here on earth.**

THANKSGIVING AND COMMUNION

OFFERING PRAYER *(Ephesians 5, John 9, 1 Samuel 16)*
    All-seeing God, you see the gifts we have given
        and the offering we are giving:
        our treasure and our time,
        our service and our lives.
    Help us perceive the value of your gifts you,
        and the ways our generous sharing
            brings your realm more closely to this earth.
    Bless our lives and our gifts,
        that they might become points of light
            to bring all of creation closer to you
                and to your love. Amen.

MARCH 15, 2026

SENDING FORTH

BENEDICTION (Psalm 23, Ephesians 5)
As Christ's light has led us here,
so now Christ's light leads us into the world.
Go with the light, go to be light.
We will brighten the world with God's love.

Notes

March 22, 2026

Fifth Sunday in Lent

Mary Boyd

COLOR
Purple

SCRIPTURE READINGS
Ezekiel 37:1-14; Psalm 130; Romans 8:6-11; John 11:1-45

THEME IDEAS
It appears that death has conquered. Dry bones lie on the valley floor and Lazarus is dead in his tomb. Yet out of death and despair, God calls forth life. As wait and we hope, the Spirit of God summons new life and peace.

INVITATION AND GATHERING

CENTERING WORDS (Psalm 130)
In the quiet, we wait for you, O God. We hope for your transforming love. In the darkness of despair, we trust that you are here.

CALL TO WORSHIP (Ezekiel 37, Psalm 130)
Everything seems dead.
There is no life anywhere.

Our hopes have perished.
   We see no future.
Send the power of your spirit upon us.
   Breathe new life into us.
We wait for your transforming love.
   We hope. We wait. We trust.

~or~

CALL TO WORSHIP (Psalm 130)
   Cry out to God.
      God listens to us.
   Hope in God.
      God forgives us.
   Wait for God.
      God's love is faithful.

OPENING PRAYER (Ezekiel 37, Psalm 130, John 11)
   Come, Spirit of God.
   We wait for your presence.
   We trust in your abiding promises.
   Breathe the breath of your power into us this day,
      that we may experience the power of new life,
         the promise of forgiveness,
            and blessing of community. Amen.

PROCLAMATION AND RESPONSE

PRAYER OF YEARNING (Ezekiel 37, Psalm 130)
   We cry to you, O God.
   It is so easy to be overwhelmed with all that is going on.
   It is so hard to see any hope.
   Everywhere we look, we see struggles and loss.
   We feel we have failed.
   But where we see death,
      you breathe new life.
   Where we see failure,
      your forgiving love changes everything.

You alone, O God, have the power
    to bring forth new life, new hope,
        and new beginnings.
Be with us as we wait for you.
Teach us to place our trust in your faithful love. Amen.

~or~

PRAYER OF YEARNING (Psalm 130)
Sometimes the night seems so long.
We lie there, waiting for morning,
    waiting for the first glimpse of light.
In the same way, we wait for you, O God.
We long to know that you are there
    and that you care about us.
Help us trust your faithful love.
Encourage us as we wait for your promises. Amen.

WORDS OF ASSURANCE (John 11:25)
Jesus promises, "I am the resurrection and the life.
Whoever trusts in me will live."
Let us trust the promise of new life.

~or~

WORDS OF ASSURANCE (Psalm 130)
God promises forgiveness.
We wait in hope, placing our trust in God's word.

PASSING THE PEACE OF CHRIST (Romans 8)
The Spirit draws us out of ourselves and helps us see others as beloved children of God. The Spirit leads us to life and peace. Let us celebrate the Spirit we see in each other.

PRAYER OF PREPARATION (Romans 8)
Spirit of God, breathe your power into our hearts, that we may hear your word for us today.

RESPONSE TO THE WORD *(John 11)*
    When the cords of death bind us,
        Jesus says, "Unbind them."
    May the power of those words
        free us from all that keeps us from living fully
        in the love of God and the grace of Christ.

THANKSGIVING AND COMMUNION

INVITATION TO THE OFFERING *(Ezekiel 37, Psalm 130)*
    God breathes new life into us, giving us hope. We can trust God's promises. Grateful for God's presence, we bring our gifts this day.

OFFERING PRAYER *(Ezekiel 37)*
    Spirit of God, you breathe new life
        into the dead and stuck places of our daily living.
    We are so grateful for the power
        of your transforming love.
    We bring these gifts,
        hoping that they will breathe new life
            into barren places of our world.
    We bring our lives, filled with new life,
        ready to serve all your creation.

SENDING FORTH

BENEDICTION *(Ezekiel 37)*
    Where there seems to be no life,
        God breathes new life.
    Where there is no hope,
        God comes with new possibilities.
    Go forth into the world,
        knowing that God is at work in every place.
    Feel the breath of God blowing peace and new life
        into our kingdom building.

Notes

March 29, 2026

Palm/Passion Sunday

Mary Scifres
Copyright © Mary Scifres

COLOR
Purple

PALM SUNDAY READINGS
Psalm 118:1-2, 19-29; Matthew 21:1-11

PASSION SUNDAY READINGS
Isaiah 50:4-9a; Psalm 31:9-16; Philippians 2:5-11; Matthew 26:14–27:66 (27:11-54)

THEME IDEAS
Such a contrast to integrate both the celebration of Jesus' entry of palms and parades into Jerusalem with the impending betrayals, trial, torture, and crucifixion! For today's entry, we focus on the celebration of Palm Sunday, tinged as it is with the shadows that lie ahead. For more specific Passion Sunday ideas, please consult the Good Friday entry or *The Abingdon Worship Annual 2020* and 2023.

INVITATION AND GATHERING

CENTERING WORDS *(Matthew 21)*
Everyone loves a parade—until they don't. Even as we wave our palms, we know that many lined the streets with jeers, not cheers. May our words of blessing and hope ring strongly, even when faced with the jeers and cruelty of the world.

CALL TO WORSHIP *(Matthew 21, Psalm 118)*
Give thanks to God, who is truly good.
Hosanna in the highest!
Praise Christ, whose love abounds with grace.
Hosanna in the highest!
Welcome the Spirit with songs of praise.
Hosanna in the highest!

OPENING PRAYER *(Matthew 21, Isaiah 50)*
Christ of both celebration and sorrow,
 be with us in our time of worship today
 and in the week ahead.
Help us embrace the fullness of your story,
 both the triumph and the tragedy.
Strengthen us to proclaim blessing and hope,
 no matter the circumstances,
  that we may be children of your promise,
  both now and forevermore. Amen.

PROCLAMATION AND RESPONSE

PRAYER OF YEARNING
Faithful One, we want to be as faithful to you
 as you are to us.
Help us sing your praises joyously and proudly,
 even when the jeering crowds frighten us.
Walk with us in moments of celebration
 and times of trouble.

Guide our steps, save our lives,
> and help us bring your message of love to the world.

Hosanna, O faithful One; hosanna in the highest. Amen.

WORDS OF ASSURANCE *(Psalm 118)*
Rejoice and be glad, for God's steadfast love
> endures forever!

PASSING THE PEACE OF CHRIST *(Matthew 21)*
Blessed are you, for you come in God's name.
> **Blessed are you, for you come in God's name.**

Let's share signs of blessing and love
as we pass the peace of Christ on this holy day.

INTRODUCTION TO THE WORD *(Psalm 118)*
This is the Lord's gate, God's word, a foundation we can trust. Let's listen for the firm foundation of God's holy word.

RESPONSE TO THE WORD *(Matthew 21, Matthew 26-27, Palm Sunday, Passion)*
Even as we sing our praise,
> **we know that this is a week of deep sorry.**

Triumph turns to tragedy
before tragedy can turn to triumph.
> **Yet, we embrace the joy of this day.**

It is strength for the journey ahead.
> **May our joy and God's blessings
> give us endurance.**

We will need it to face the pain of Holy week.
> **Help us meet the reality of our lives
> and the needs of our world.**

THANKSGIVING AND COMMUNION

INVITATION TO THE OFFERING *(Philippians 2)*
May Christ's values of generosity, grace, and love guide our giving of time, talent and treasure. May these values become the focus of our thoughts during this time of offering.

OFFERING PRAYER (Psalm 118)
>We give you thanks, Christ Jesus,
>>for your goodness and your grace.
>Blessing the gifts and lives we offer to you,
>>that they may bring goodness and grace
>>>to your world.
>In gratitude and joy, we pray. Amen.

PRAYER OF CONSECRATION (Matthew 21, Psalm 118, Philippians 2)
>Pour out your Holy Spirit
>>on these gifts of bread and wine,
>>>for they remind us that your life and love
>>>>flow through us each and every time
>>>>>we call upon your name.
>Bless us with your Spirit,
>>that we may be blessings
>>>of your grace and goodness,
>>>>woven together in your love.
>May we be one with you,
>>one with each other,
>>>and one in ministry for all the world.
>Hosanna, Holy One! Amen.

SENDING FORTH

BENEDICTION (Psalm 118, Matthew 21, Matthew 26–27)
>With songs in our heart,
>>**we move toward the cross.**
>May God bless us
>>**with strength for the journey ahead.**
>Go with God,
>>**knowing Christ is on the journey with us.**

MARCH 29, 2026

Notes

April 2, 2026

Holy Thursday

Amy Hunter

COLOR
Purple

SCRIPTURE READINGS
Exodus 12:1-4, (5-10), 11-14; Psalm 116:1-2, 12-19;
1 Corinthians 11:23-26; John 13:1-17, 31b -35

THEME IDEAS
Worship on Holy Thursday invites God's people to take a first step into the terror, mystery, and exaltation of Jesus' death and resurrection. The readings reverberate with ritual. We hear the foundational stories for the feasts of the Passover and Unleavened Bread, the institution of Holy Communion, and the new commandment that we love one another as Jesus loves us. As worshipers, we are expected to know, remember, and even lean into the context of these stories—the coming Exodus, the imminent crucifixion, and the disciples' unfolding betrayal and abandonment. The Triduum invites us to go beyond observing a ritual or hearing an old, old story. As we make these solemn days of Holy Thursday, Good Friday, and Holy Saturday our own stories, we journey with Christ toward Easter.

APRIL 2, 2026

INVITATION AND GATHERING

CENTERING WORDS (John 13)
Jesus loves those who are his own and loves them till the end. We belong to Jesus. We are his own.

CALL TO WORSHIP (Exodus 12, Psalm 116,
1 Corinthians 11, John 13)
God's beloved in Jesus Christ, we gather in worship,
remembering all that God has done for us.
Now the Son of Man has been glorified,
and God has been glorified in him.
Remember the Passover of the Lord,
which made time and history new for God's people.
Now the Son of Man has been glorified,
and God has been glorified in him.
Remember Jesus' commandment to live a new way,
loving one another as he has loved us.
Now the Son of Man has been glorified,
and God has been glorified in him.
Remember the bread broken and given,
the cup of new allegiance with God.
Now the Son of Man has been glorified,
and God has been glorified in him.
God's beloved in Jesus Christ, God has given us
everything! Come and worship.
We belong to Jesus. We are his own. Amen.

OPENING PRAYER (1 Corinthians 11, John 13)
Holy God who holds nothing back
to draw us to yourself,
be with us as we tell the story
of Jesus sharing a final meal with his friends
before his death.
Nurture us as we repeat the sacred words
used since the beginning of your Church.

We will bless bread and cup in remembrance of Jesus,
> who gave himself for us
>> and calls us to a new life of love.

On this Holy Thursday, may we know the mystery
> of time past, present, and future—
>> time met together in your gracious love.

We celebrate your saving presence
> told in stories throughout human history.

We hear your commandment, always new and urgent,
> to make our love for one another
>> the sign of who we are as your people now.

Eating the bread and drinking the cup of your grace,
> we proclaim our hope in the eternal feast
>> where all will gather in love at your table.

May we hold nothing back as we enter together
> into this holy time. Amen.

PROCLAMATION AND RESPONSE

PRAYER OF YEARNING (Psalm 116, 1 Corinthians 11, John 13)

Jesus, even as we enter the heartbreak and anguish of Holy Week, we know that we do not fully understand what God has done for us.
> **You have loosed our bonds. What shall we return to you for all we have received?**

Sometimes we follow rituals but miss their meaning. Sometimes we say the words but forget to love.
> **May God help us pay our vows in the presence of all God's people.**

Jesus, washing the feet of your friends, you ask: "Do you know what I have done for you?"
> **May God help us to serve one another in love as you have served us.**

Jesus, breaking the bread and blessing the cup, you ask:
"Do you know what I have done for you?"
**May God help us eat and drink in remembrance
of you.**
Jesus, commanding us to love one another, you ask:
"Do you know what I have done for you?"
**We love God, who hears our every supplication.
We call on the name of the Lord.**

WORDS OF ASSURANCE (Psalm 116, John 13)
God always hears us.
We call on God as long as we live, sure of God's love.
Jesus loves those who are his own,
    loving them till the end.
Know that you are God's own beloved in Jesus Christ.

PASSING THE PEACE OF CHRIST (John 13)
Jesus says to us, "Just as I have loved you, you also should love one another." Let us greet one another with the peace of Christ's love for us.

INTRODUCTION TO THE WORD (Exodus 12, John 13)
God's beloved in Jesus Christ, the people of Israel received the Passover of the Lord as a new beginning of time and identity, and the disciples received the commandment to love one another as a new way of being God's people. In the same way, let us hear these words of scripture as God's invitation to us here and now to find new life in Jesus Christ.

RESPONSE TO THE WORD (1 Corinthians 11)
God's beloved in Jesus Christ, hear God's word
calling us to ancient practices and to new life in Christ.
**We receive from the Lord what has been handed
down to us of old.**

THANKSGIVING AND COMMUNION

INVITATION TO THE OFFERING (Psalm 116)
What shall we return to God in response
for all God's bounty to us?
**Let us offer our thanksgiving
and call on the name of God.**

OFFERING PRAYER (Psalm 116, John 13)
Holy God, whose loving presence with humanity
is beyond our comprehension,
  receive and bless the gifts we offer you today.
We give you thanks and we gather as your own people,
  to pay our vows of love to you and for one another.
Use these offerings to fulfill Jesus' commandment
  to love one another as signs of your divine love
    for the world.
We pray in the name of Jesus,
  who offers all on our behalf. Amen.

INVITATION TO COMMUNION
On Holy Thursday we remember Jesus' last meal with his friends, and we look ahead to the next two days when we will remember the Passion and the tomb. Help us to do more than simply remember these events. Help us to live them here and now as your own people—people Jesus loves now and to the end.

May this Holy Thursday be a day of remembrance.
We celebrate it as a festival to our God.

SENDING FORTH

BENEDICTION (1 Corinthians 11, John 13)
Even as he faced betrayal and death,
Jesus washed his disciples' feet

and gathered at the table with them,
loving them and inviting them to love one another.
**Now the Son of Man has been glorified,
and God has been glorified in him.**
In the name of God the Father, to whom Jesus knew
he was going as he faced his Passion;
in the name of Jesus, who loved his own
who were in the world and loved them to the end;
in the name of the Holy Spirit, who gives us the power
to fulfill Jesus' commandment that we love as he loves,
let us go forth to walk with Jesus to his cross.
We belong to Jesus. We are his own. Amen.

Notes

April 3, 2026

Good Friday

LeighAnn Shaw

COLOR
Black or None

SCRIPTURE READINGS
Isaiah 52:13–53:12; Psalm 22; Hebrews 10:16-25; John 18:1–19:42

THEME IDEAS
Hope in sacrifice. Although there is fear and trembling, forgiveness is assured. Death is never the end with our story, for our God is faithful, even amid death and despair.

INVITATION AND GATHERING

CENTERING WORDS (Hebrews 10)
Our faith holds fast to hope without wavering. Our God is faithful.

CALL TO WORSHIP (John 18–19)
On this Good Friday, we gather to remember
the crucifixion of our Lord Jesus Christ.
Amid sorrow, we seek the hope his sacrifice brings.

APRIL 3, 2026

**We come with heavy hearts, yet we hold on
to the hope that Christ's love and sacrifice
bring to the world.**
Jesus said, "When I am lifted up from the earth,
I will draw all people to myself." In His death,
we find the promise of new life and redemption.
**We look to the cross, not only as a symbol
of suffering but as a beacon of hope and salvation.**
Though we mourn today, we remember that darkness
does not have the final word. Through Jesus,
light and hope prevail.
**We stand in faith, knowing that Christ's sacrifice
opens the way to everlasting hope and life.**

Let us pray. Gracious God, as we reflect on the depth
of Jesus' sacrifice, fill our hearts with hope.
May his love guide us and his hope sustain us.
Amen.

PROCLAMATION AND RESPONSE

PRAYER OF CONFESSION (John 18–19)
Merciful God, like the disciples before us,
    we too have denied and betrayed you
        in our fear and weakness.
We have failed to stand by your truth,
    choosing self-preservation over faithfulness.
Forgive our silence in the face of injustice,
    our indifference to suffering,
        and the times we have turned away
            from your love.
In your mercy, restore us.
Help us follow Jesus' path of sacrificial love,
    that we may live as people of courage
        and compassion.
In the name of the one who loves us, we pray. Amen.

WORDS OF ASSURANCE (John 18–19)
While we turned away from God, silently complicit,
Christ died that we may live.
Through Christ, we are forgiven.
This is our hope and our good news.
It is good news indeed.
We are forgiven, even on this night. Amen.

PASSING OF THE PEACE (John 18–19)
In the darkest moments, when betrayal and fear
seemed to triumph, Jesus still spoke peace.
His peace is not just the absence of conflict
but the presence of love, even when it's hard.
Today, as we remember the struggle and sacrifice,
let's embrace the peace that defies the darkness.
We receive and share this peace with the
commitment to be bearers of love and light.
The peace of Christ is with us, breaking through
the shadows.
And it is also with you.
Let's pass this radical, life-giving peace to one another.

RESPONSE TO THE WORD (Hebrews 10)
God's Word, a message of hope and sacrifice.
We give thanks for God's Word. Amen.

THANKSGIVING AND COMMUNION

INVITATION TO THE OFFERING (John 18–19)
As we gather to reflect on the immenseness of this evening, and as we are reminded of Christ' sacrifice for us, let us respond faithfully. Consider how you can give of yourself—your time, talents and resources—to bless others and serve the Lord of Love.

OFFERING PRAYER (John 18–19)
Gracious God, we bring our offerings
as tokens of gratitude and humble commitment
for the sacrifice of your Son, Jesus Christ.

Use these gifts to spread love, bring comfort,
    and offer hope to those in need.
Bless these offerings and those who give them
    to the glory of your name. Amen.

SENDING FORTH

BENEDICTION
    The darkness of the moment is upon us.
    Although there is hope, the emptiness of death
        is overwhelming.
    The first disciples were covered in fear.
    We join those disciples haunted by the pain
        of Jesus' death.
    Go into the night and feel the darkness.
    Go out into the night and feel the loss.
    Go now into the dis-ease to wait for peace and rest.

Notes

April 5, 2026

Easter Sunday

B. J. Beu
Copyright © B. J. Beu

COLOR
White

SCRIPTURE READINGS
Acts 10:34-43; Psalm 118:1-2, 14-24; Colossians 3:1-4; John 20:1-18 (or Matthew 28:1-10)

THEME IDEAS
The steadfast love spoken of by the psalmist has raised Jesus from the dead. How will we recognize our risen savior? Jesus calls each of us by name—a call to discipleship and service. The hymn, "Christ the Lord Is Risen Today" says it all. Everything else is commentary. Yet, before we give ourselves over to Easter celebration, reflect on the hopelessness and defeat that Mary and the disciples felt as they came to the tomb. Beginning the service in near darkness with the cross still shrouded with the black cloth of Good Friday is an effective way to capture the surprising truth that death does not have the final word.

APRIL 5, 2026

INVITATION AND GATHERING

CENTERING WORDS
Easter teaches us that life never ends and love never dies.

WORSHIP OPENING AND CALL TO WORSHIP *(John 20)*
(Begin the service in near darkness, with only a cross shrouded in black cloth on the altar/Lord's Table. Ring a bell or singing bowl three times.)

(Read John 20:1-13a with "What Wondrous Love Is This" or similar tune played softly underneath until end of reading. After music ends ring sing bowl twice.)

> We don't know where to find Jesus.
> **The days have been dark.**
> **The news has been sad.**
> We don't know what to do with our grief.
> **The cross has claimed his life.**
> **The tomb has shrouded our hope.**
> We don't know where to turn for comfort.
> **Who has stolen him from us?**
> **Why are we alone at the tomb?**
> We don't know where to look for answers.
> **Tears and sorrow blind us in our grief.**
> **We don't know where to find Jesus.**

(Ring sing bowl twice. Then read John 20:13b-18 while acolyte or dancer brings lit Pascal Candle forward and places it upon the altar/Lord's Table while "Now the Green Blade Rises" or similar tune is played underneath the scripture reading. After music ends, ring bell or singing bowl three times.)

OPENING PRAYER or PRAYER OF YEARNING *(John 20, Acts 10)*
> God of mystery and might,
>> on a dawn shrouded in grief and pain,
>>> you surprise us with the light
>>>> of your wondrous love.

We come to the tomb expecting death,
    but find life instead.
Take us back to that moment,
    when fear was healed by hope
        and death was banished by life.
In the holy awe of Easter morning,
    may our sing out our joy,
        for Christ, our Lord, has risen today! Amen.

(Sing "Christ the Lord has Risen Today")

CHILDREN'S MOMENT
(Before the service, hide the Easter Lilies among the pews or choir loft. During the Children's Moment, send the youth on a hunt to find the flowers, and then use them to decorate the worship space.)

PROCLAMATION AND RESPONSE

PASTORAL PRAYER and LORD'S PRAYER (John 20, Acts 10)
(Consider using a thought-provoking version of the Lord's Prayer, like the one below from The New Zealand Book of Common Prayer*)*

Source of resurrection joy,
    breathe new life into us this holy morning.
Open our hearts to the mystery of this day,
    for we long to touch the depth of your mercy
        and the vastness of your boundless love.
From the darkness of doubt,
    you have led us into your glorious light
        of faith and love.
Truly, you reveal at Easter that life never ends
    and love never dies.
And so we join with Christians around the world,
    as we pray the prayer that your Son taught us:

Eternal Spirit,
    Earth-maker, Pain-bearer, Life-giver,
    Source of all that is and that shall be,
    Father and Mother of us all,
    Loving God, in whom is heaven:
The hallowing of your name
    echoes through the universe!
The way of your justice be followed
    by the peoples of the world!
Your heavenly will be done by all created beings!
Your commonwealth of peace and freedom
    sustain our hope and come on earth.
With the bread we need for today, feed us.
In the hurts we absorb from one another, forgive us.
In times of temptation and testing, strengthen us.
From trials too great to endure, spare us.
From the grip of all that is evil, free us.
For you reign in the glory of the power that is love,
    now and forever. Amen.

PASSING THE PEACE OF CHRIST (Psalm 118, John 20)
    With overflowing joy and boundless gratitude for new life in Christ, let us share the triumph of love over hate as we exchange signs of Christ's peace this blessed day.

RESPONSE TO THE WORD (Psalm 118)
    This is the day that the Lord has made.
    Let us rejoice and be glad in it.
    This is the life that our God has brought.
    Let us sing out and be glad in it.
    This is the light that our savior shines forth.
    Let us give thanks and be glad in it.
    This is the love that has conquered the grave.
    Let us rejoice and be glad in it.

THANKSGIVING AND COMMUNION

OFFERING PRAYER *(Acts 10)*
    With gratitude and joy, O God,
        we bring these gifts for your use,
            even as we offer our very lives
                into your loving service.
    May our financial assistance
        and the ministries of this church
            bring new life to a hurting world
                in need of resurrection.
    May our gifts touch the lost and lonely
        with the assurance that in your arms,
            life never ends and love never dies. Amen.

SENDING FORTH

BENEDICTION *(John 20)*
    From darkness and death,
    we find light and life.
        Christ is risen! Alleluia!
    From doubt and despair,
    we find faith and hope.
        Christ is with us now! Shout for joy!
    From dead ends and overgrown paths,
    we find new beginnings and clear vistas.
        Christ is risen! Christ is risen indeed!

APRIL 5, 2026

Notes

April 12, 2026

Second Sunday of Easter

Rebecca Gaudino

COLOR
White

SCRIPTURE READINGS
Acts 2:14a, 22-32; Psalm 16; 1 Peter 1:3-9; John 20:19-31

THEME IDEAS

Why does Thomas want to *touch* Jesus' wounds? Yes, he wants proof that this living person before him is the Jesus who died. But what if there is something more? To see *and touch* Jesus' wounded body is for Thomas to experience an embodied knowing of Jesus' suffering—his torn and bruised flesh. The disciples do not know firsthand Jesus' last hours, except for John and the three Marys who stood at the foot of the cross. Only Joseph of Arimathea and Nicodemus wrapped Jesus' body and placed it in a tomb. No wonder then that Jesus pronounces "Peace be with you" three times in eleven verses to fearful disciples who have heard the reports of his death but now see his wounds. You could say that Jesus shows them the suffering of our world in his own body. And when he invites Thomas to touch his wounds (perhaps Thomas does so), he invites him to touch this suffering and then to recognize

APRIL 12, 2026

and claim the incredible power of God in Jesus: "My Lord and my God!" (John 20:28, NRSVue). From this power, disciples like Thomas turn around and, as Jesus did, touch the wounds of the world through the power of the Holy Spirit. Maybe this story is why some Christians have believed for centuries that Thomas journeyed all the way to the Malabar Coast of India to tend to the wounds of what Jesus elsewhere calls "the least of these" (Matthew 25:40)!

INVITATION AND GATHERING

CENTERING WORDS (Psalm 16)
In you I take refuge. In you I find life. May I keep you always before me.

CALL TO WORSHIP (Psalm 16, John 20)
Voice 1	You who have touched the wounds of the world,
Voice 2	*You who have been wounded by the world,*
All	**Jesus Christ, our Lord and our God,**
Voice 1	we have not seen you, Risen One.
Voice 2	*We have not touched you,*
All	**but we believe you are our Lord and our God.**
Voice 1	You are our refuge in hurt and pain.
Voice 2	*You are the path of life.*
All	**You are our Lord and our God! Alleluia!**

OPENING PRAYER (John 20)
Jesus of the Cross, Jesus of the Resurrection,
   we rejoice in you.
For long before the experience of the cross,
   you defeated the powers of sin, pain, and death
     in the hurting people around you.
And then *you* were struck down.
But you defeated the cross and stood
   before your beloved disciples,
     as you are present today—alive again.

We rejoice in you, Risen Savior, for you open before us
  your life-giving peace and power.
You are our Lord and our God.
Alleluia! Amen.

PROCLAMATION AND RESPONSE

PRAYER OF YEARNING (Psalm 16, John 20)
  Jesus Christ, our Brother, our Savior,
    sometimes we are bold and sure
      that you are the Living One who defeated death
        and destruction for us all.
  Sometimes we wonder at the ancient stories
    of your resurrection, and we are not so sure
      that things happened the way stories tell them.
  Amid our doubts, bless us with your peace.
  Bless us with the joy and assurance of your presence,
    wherever we are in our journey of faith.
  In your compassionate name, we pray. Amen.

WORDS OF ASSURANCE or PASSING THE PEACE OF CHRIST (Psalm 16, John 20)
  "Peace be with you!" Jesus said to his disciples, both those who saw and believed *and* the one who questioned. Today Jesus Christ also bestows his peace and presence upon us: "Peace be with you!" Amen.

PASSING THE PEACE OF CHRIST (John 20)
  Long ago, Jesus Christ gave his peace to disciples who were locked in a room and sorely in need of peace. Let us pass this peace to all who join us today with the words, "Peace be with you!"

RESPONSE TO THE WORD (Psalm 16, John 20)
  Jesus Christ, our Lord and our God,
    you have touched the wounds of the world
    and have been wounded by the world.

We too claim your living power in our lives
   and for the sake of the world.
Like you, may we touch the wounds of those who suffer
   in body, mind, and spirit,
      that your triumph over death may become the path
      of life for them.
Remembering the marks of the nails
   and the piercing of the sword,
      we pray that this part of your story may heal us,
      even as it wounded you.
We rejoice that you prevailed over the powers of sin,
   death, and destruction. Alleluia! Amen.

THANKSGIVING AND COMMUNION

INVITATION TO THE OFFERING *(Psalm 16, John 20)*
   We are blessed with what the psalmist calls a "goodly heritage." We are disciples and heirs in the family of Jesus Christ, our Lord and our God. Let us give generously, so that others may know the faithfulness of Jesus, alive in our lives, alive in their lives, the very source of healing, joy, and delight.

OFFERING PRAYER *(Psalm 16, John 20)*
   Jesus our Protector and Savior,
      we thank you for every gift you have given us
         that brings us delight and joy in this life.
   We thank you for every gift that comes to us
      in times of despair to lift us up
         and tend to our sorrows.
   May these gifts reach out to our world,
      that others may know your joy, your caring,
         your deep understanding of despair—
            and your Life that-defeats death. Amen.

SENDING FORTH

BENEDICTION (John 20)
    Jesus called out to his disciples, "Peace be with you!"
        We praise Jesus, our Lord and our God,
        for this peace.
    Jesus breathed upon the disciples
    [*breathe out so all can hear*] and said,
    "Receive the Holy Spirit!"
        We praise Jesus, our Lord and our God,
        for the Holy Spirit who accompanies us.
    As disciples of Jesus Christ, go out into the world
    with power—to forgive, to touch wounds
    with healing hands, and to live out the love, life,
    and power of our Lord and our God.
        Alleluia! Amen.

Notes

April 19, 2026

Third Sunday of Easter

B. J. Beu
Copyright © B. J. Beu

COLOR

White

SCRIPTURE READINGS

Acts 2:14a, 36-41; Psalm 116:1-4, 12-19; 1 Peter 1:17-23; Luke 24:13-35

THEME IDEAS

Luke's story of the walk to Emmaus carries so many beautiful themes: Christ walks with us, even when we are unaware of his presence; Christ stays with us when we offer hospitality to strangers; Christ opens our eyes to the presence of the divine when we break bread together. Acts invites us to respond to Christ's gifts by being baptized with power of the Holy Spirit. The psalmist praises God for rescue, promising faithful service in return. The epistle speaks of mutual love that is born in our hearts as we respond to Christ. Christ meets us, even when we don't recognize him; then Christ opens our eyes and offers us a glorious future. This is good news indeed.

INVITATION AND GATHERING

CENTERING WORDS (*Luke 24*)
>Easter invites us to be ready to meet Christ, anywhere, at any time, in anyone.

CALL TO WORSHIP (*Psalm 116, 1 Peter 1, Luke 24*)
>Even if we feel abandoned and alone,
>>**Christ meets us here.**
>
>Even when we become lost and disoriented,
>>**Christ rescues us in our need.**
>
>Even when our hearts are touched by the frost,
>>**Christ warms our spirits.**
>
>Even when all light has faded to black,
>>**Christ illumines our Way.**
>
>Here in this house of worship
>enter, rejoice, and come home.

OPENING PRAYER (*Luke 24*)
>Lover of our souls, you meet us on the road of life
>>and lift us from our pain and grief.
>
>Heal our hardness of heart,
>>and open our minds to the subtleness of your ways
>>>and the grandeur of your kingdom.
>
>During times of suffering and doubt,
>>help us grow strong and true,
>>>through your enduring word.
>
>Reveal your presence to us,
>>as we show hospitality to strangers
>>>and break bread in your name. Amen.

PROCLAMATION AND RESPONSE

PRAYER OF YEARNING (*Luke 24*)
>God of Easter hope, when our gaze is cast within,
>it is easy to miss your presence in our midst.

When we fail to recognize you on the road,
    touch our minds with your wisdom and truth,
        and set our hearts on fire with your holy love.
During times of confusion and doubt,
    open our eyes to your life-giving presence,
    and rekindle our Easter faith. Amen.

WORDS OF ASSURANCE (1 Peter 1)
In the resurrection of Jesus, we find hope
    and an imperishable seed of faith.
Risen with Christ, we are born anew.

PASSING THE PEACE OF CHRIST (Luke 24)
Welcome Christ as a fellow traveler on the journey of life. As you share signs of his peace with one another, see his eyes looking back at you.

INVITATION TO THE WORD (Luke 24)
Risen Lord, speak to us this day,
    that our hearts may burn within us.
Reveal anew the mystery and the power
    of your glorious resurrection.

RESPONSE TO THE WORD (Psalm 116, Luke 24)
Lift your eyes and look around.
Behold the Lord in our midst.
    Our hearts burn within us
    when he speaks to our secret hearts.
Lift the cup of salvation
and call on God's holy name.
    The Lord hears our cries
    and answers our prayers.
Lift your hearts to Lord of life
who meets us in our need.
    The Lord hears our vows of faithful love
    and purifies our souls through obedience
    to God's enduring word.

THANKSGIVING AND COMMUNION

INVITATION TO THE OFFERING (Psalm 116)
What shall we return to the Lord for God's many gifts? What praises shall we sing to honor God's manifold blessings? In the presence of God's people, let us pay our vows to the Lord with heartfelt gratitude.

OFFERING PRAYER (Psalm 116, Luke 24)
Loving God, you come to us in moments of grief
    when we have lost our ability
        to perceive your presence.
Receive our thanks for meeting us on the road
    and for quickening our spirits.
Receive our praise for opening your word to us
    and for enlightening our minds.
May the gifts we bring before you now
    reflect the stirring our hearts,
        as you heal the broken places in our lives.
May the offering we bring forth
    stir the hearts of those in need
        of your mercy and your grace. Amen.

COMMUNION PRAYER (1 Peter 1, Luke 24)
Walk with us, O traveler unknown,
    and open our hearts and minds
        to the mystery of your ways.
Reveal to us your holy presence
    in the breaking of the bread
        and in the sharing of the cup.
Bring us fullness of life in your name,
    that we might be a people of mutual love,
        born of your gracious love and mercy.
Amen.

APRIL 19, 2026

SENDING FORTH

BENEDICTION (*Luke 24*)
  As you meet strangers on the road,
  learn to recognize Christ in your mist.
  **As our hearts burn within us,
  we will recognize his whispers to our souls.**
  As you experience Christ in the smile of another,
  share the love of God with one another.
  **As the scales fall from our eyes,
  we will see Easter miracles all around us.**
  Go with God's blessings.

Notes

April 26, 2026

Fourth Sunday of Easter

B. J. Beu
Copyright © B. J. Beu

COLOR
   White

SCRIPTURE READINGS
   Acts 2:42-47; Psalm 23; 1 Peter 2:19-25; John 10:1-10

THEME IDEAS
   The shepherd that is revered by the psalmist is celebrated by John as both shepherd and gate for the sheep. We rejoice that Jesus, our shepherd, calls us each by name and is the one who came that we may have abundant life. Acts describes abundant life as a gifts of Christian fellowship, breaking bread together, prayer, attention to the apostle's teachings, and sharing all things in common. How far we have moved from that early paradigm of selfless giving! But when we return to our shepherd and guardian after going astray, the epistle says we are healed and welcomed home.

INVITATION AND GATHERING

CENTERING WORDS *(Psalm 23, John 10)*
   Listen, our shepherd is calling us by name.

APRIL 26, 2026

CALL TO WORSHIP (Psalm 23, John 10)
    The Lord is our shepherd.
    We are Christ's sheep.
    The shepherd shelters us in green pastures.
    In Christ, we dwell secure.
    The shepherd nourishes us and restores our souls.
    Christ is our shepherd and gate to the Most High.

~or~

CALL TO WORSHIP (Psalm 23, John 10)
    Do you need a guide?
    The Lord is our shepherd.
    Do you need a path to new life?
    The Lord is our gate.
    Do you need rest?
    The Lord restores our souls.
    Come, let us worship.

OPENING PRAYER (John 10)
    Loving Shepherd, you call us as your own.
    When danger is close at hand,
        you gather us to yourself,
            that we might dwell secure.
    When evil surrounds us,
        you give us a home and a safe place to rest.
    When foes threaten our fellowship,
        you rescue us from peril.
    Restore our souls, Gentle Savior,
        and lead us in the paths of righteousness,
            that we may walk in the ways
                of goodness and mercy,
                    all the days of our lives. Amen.

PROCLAMATION AND RESPONSE

PRAYER OF YEARNING (Psalm 23, John 10)
    Loving Shepherd, even when we stray,
        we long to be gathered to your side.
    Even when we strive to find our own way,
        we yearn to return to your fold
            and rest secure in your gentle arms.
    Even when we bleat our resistance,
        we seek your guidance and direction in our lives.
    Be our gate, our way to safe havens,
        where we can always find our way home
            and dwell secure in your love. Amen.

WORDS OF ASSURANCE (Psalm 23)
    The Good Shepherd anoints our heads with oil,
        nourishes us with living waters,
        delivers us from evil,
        and watches over us day and night.
    Because of our Shepherd, we shall dwell
        in the house of the Lord forever.

PASSING THE PEACE OF CHRIST (Psalm 23, John 10)
    The peace of our shepherd passes all understanding. Let us share signs of this peace with one another as we dwell secure in Christ's flock.

RESPONSE TO THE WORD (Psalm 23, John 10, 1 Peter 2)
    Keeper of our souls, call us back to you flock
        when we go astray.
    You are ever our shepherd and our guardian.
    May your words of life resonate within us
        like a drum in the valley,
            and may its echo never fade. Amen.

CALL TO PRAYER (Acts 2)
The early disciples devoted themselves to prayer, the teachings of the apostles, and sharing the bread of life. They were a people of prayer—a people who shared their joys and concerns, their sorrows and passions with one another and with the Lord. Come, let us follow their example and lift our prayers to God.

THANKSGIVING AND COMMUNION

OFFERING PRAYER (Psalm 23, John 10)
Shepherd of our souls, we thank you for the love
    that flows through our lives.
May this love flow through these gifts,
    that no one may be in need.
Work through this offering and through our very lives,
    that your community of love
        may be established here on earth
            for all the sheep of your fold.
In your holy name, we pray. Amen.

SENDING FORTH

BENEDICTION (Psalm 23, John 10)
The Lord is our shepherd.
We shall not want.
In pastures green, we rest secure.
By still waters, we rest secure.
Go with the blessings of our shepherd.

Notes

May 3, 2026

Fifth Sunday of Easter

Mary Scifres
Copyright © Mary Scifres

COLOR

White

SCRIPTURE READINGS

Acts 7:55-60; Psalm 31:1-5, 15-16; 1 Peter 2:2-10; John 14:1-14

THEME IDEAS

God's steadfast faithfulness makes our faithfulness possible. We need not be the strong ones, for God's strength is enough: to give Stephen courage to face martyrdom; to give the psalmist faith to proclaim God's refuge, even when surrounded by enemies; and to give Peter faith to prophesy that we are being built into the house of God. Jesus knows that the troubles of this world are real; yet he promises that we can trust God to lead us on the way both in this earthly life and in the life to come. God's steadfast faithfulness will get us through, even when our faith waivers.

INVITATION AND GATHERING

CENTERING WORDS *(John 14)*
Trusting God sounds so simple, but trust is a journey. Join the journey toward trust, for Christ will show us the way.

CALL TO WORSHIP *(Acts 7, 1 Peter 2, John 14)*
Come to Christ, our cornerstone.
Christ has called us here.
Trust in God, our firm foundation.
God is with us here.
Rest in the Spirit, our peace beyond peace.
May the Spirit guide our way.

OPENING PRAYER *(Acts 7, Psalm 31, John 14)*
Faithful God, you are our refuge and our strength,
   a mighty fortress in a world of chaos and turmoil.
Protect us, but also encourage us to be brave.
Strengthen us to face this world
   and to make it a better place.
Inspire our worship,
   that in this time we may deepen our faith
      and place our trust in you. Amen.

PROCLAMATION AND RESPONSE

PRAYER OF YEARNING *(Acts 7, Psalm 31, 1 Peter 2)*
Mighty God, we want to be brave,
   but it's tempting to be small and afraid.
Lift us up when we fall down.
Protect us from our own doubts and fears.
Shine your face upon us with mercy and grace,
   that we might find the courage and strength
      to be steadfast and faithful, loving and righteous.
Be our strong foundation,
   so that we may grow up as your household,

your family, and your people of justice, love,
and mercy.
In hope and gratitude, we pray. Amen.

WORDS OF ASSURANCE *(Acts 7, Psalm 31, John 14)*
God's faithful love is true, and God's strength
is enough.
Rest in God's love and trust in God's strength,
for these gifts are all we need.

PASSING THE PEACE OF CHRIST *(1 Peter 2, John 14)*
Having received mercy and love from God, let's share mercy and love with one another—both now, as we share Christ's peace, and throughout the week ahead.

RESPONSE TO THE WORD *(Acts 7, Psalm 31, 1 Peter 2)*
God, be our refuge and strength,
an ever-faithful rock in the shifting sands of life.
Christ, be our firm foundation,
nourishing us to grow more and more like you.
Holy Spirit, be our wisdom and guide,
empowering us to be God's people in the world.

THANKSGIVING AND COMMUNION

OFFERING PRAYER *(Psalm 31, 1 Peter 2, John 14)*
God of steadfast faithfulness and love, bless these gifts,
that they may bring your message of faith and love
to the world.
Bless us also,
that we may be steadfast and true in our giving
and in our living.
Build our church, build us, and build your world
into a household of love and justice—
the household you've envisioned
since the beginning of time.
In faith and trust, we pray. Amen.

INVITATION TO COMMUNION (1 Peter 2)
Here at this table,
　　the pure milk of Christ's love is ours.
Here at this table,
　　the nourishment of God's salvation is ours.
Here at this table, the strength of the Holy Spirit is ours.
Come to be fed.
Come to be nourished.
Come to be strengthened,
　　for all are welcome at this table of grace.

SENDING FORTH

BENEDICTION (John 14)
Even as God sends us into the world,
　　Christ has prepared the way.
　　Following Christ, we go to serve and love
　　with faith and hope.

MAY 3, 2026

Notes

May 10, 2026

Sixth Sunday of Easter
Festival of the Christian Home/Mother's Day

B. J. Beu
Copyright © B. J. Beu

COLOR
White

SCRIPTURE READINGS
Acts 17:22-31; Psalm 66:8-20; 1 Peter 3:13-22; John 14:15-21

THEME IDEAS

Love and suffering seem to be the two great paths to God. Suffering gets our attention and is a great vehicle of transformation, while love shows us the nature of God. The psalmist speaks of being tested and tried as silver is tried. God put other nations over Israel to lead the Israelites through fire and water into a spacious place of blessing. The epistle speaks of the suffering that will come from following Christ, and then urges the people to do good works anyway. For it is better to suffer for doing good than for doing evil. In the Gospel reading, Jesus promises the disciples that he will not leave them comfortless, but will send them the Advocate, the Holy Spirit, to teach them the truth

MAY 10, 2026

about God and holy love. The reading from Acts does not fit this theme, but recounts the story of Paul in the Areopagus, proclaiming the God of Jesus Christ as the one the Athenians worshiped as an unknown god. Acts and the epistle also share the theme of searching and groping for God and ultimate truth.

INVITATION AND GATHERING

CENTERING WORDS *(Psalm 66, John 14)*
Through fire and testing, God brings us to a place of blessing and promise. The Holy Spirit leads us onto the great path of love.

CALL TO WORSHIP *(Acts 17, John 14)*
Gather us in, O God.
Amidst fire and storm, make us whole.
Bring us into your presence, Holy One.
From suffering and pain, save us.
Shelter us in your loving arms, Precious Lord.
On the highways of life, guide us.
Make us your disciples, Great Spirit.
As we worship this day, lead us home.

OPENING PRAYER *(Psalm 66, 1 Peter 3, John 14)*
Holy flame, burn away our fears and regrets,
 that our spirits may shine like burnished gold.
Refiner's Fire, purify our lives like precious silver,
 that our hearts may glow with holy love.
Forge of truth, mold us into vessels of compassion,
 that our lives may reveal your glory. Amen.

PROCLAMATION AND RESPONSE

PRAYER OF YEARNING *(1 Peter 3, John 14)*
Fulfiller of our lives, we yearn to embody
 your commandment of love
  and pursue what we know is right.

We long to ease the plight of others,
    even as we seek our own comfort.
Nurture our hope this day,
    as we fulfill your commandment of love,
        that we may live as your children
            and abide in your Spirit. Amen.

ASSURANCE OF PARDON (Psalm 66)
Even when we are tested by the refiner's fire,
    God brings us to a place of laughter and light
        on the other side of our trials.
The Advocate meets us in our suffering
    and heals us in holy love.

PASSING THE PEACE OF CHRIST (Psalm 66, John 14)
On the other side of trials, rest in the sanctuary of God's healing love. Come, let us share the peace of Christ with one anther—the peace promised through the Holy Spirit.

INTRODUCTION TO THE WORD (Acts 17, Psalm 66, John 14)
Search for God, seekers of the way.
    Where shall we go to find what we seek?
Grope for truth, disciples of wisdom.
    Where shall we look for answers?
Listen for the Word of God.
    We will listen with the Spirit's help.

RESPONSE TO THE WORD (1 Peter 3, John 14)
Help us hear your voice, Spirit of truth,
    that we may respond with our very lives.
Teach us your commandment of love, Gracious One,
    that we may walk in your ways
        and reveal your presence to the world. Amen.

MAY 10, 2026

THANKSGIVING AND COMMUNION

INVITATION TO THE OFFERING
    We are called to be more than hearers of the word, but doers of the word as well. Let us fulfill this calling by sharing God's love and concern with the world.

OFFERING PRAYER (Psalm 66, 1 Timothy 3)
    Refiner's fire, you purify us
        and wash us in the waters of our baptism.
    In gratitude and thanksgiving,
        we return these gifts to you now,
            that they may bring hope and light
                to a world in need. Amen.

SENDING FORTH

BENEDICTION (Acts 17, John 14)
    Once we searched and groped for God in darkness.
    Now we reside with Christ in glorious light.
    Once we lived as if God was far from us.
    Now we rejoice each day in God's presence.
    Once we strove for God's acceptance.
    Now we rest secure in God's love.

Notes

May 17, 2026

Ascension Sunday
Seventh Sunday of Easter

B. J. Beu
Copyright © B. J. Beu

COLOR
White

ASCENSION SCRIPTURE READINGS
Acts 1:1-11; Psalm 47; Ephesians 1:15-23; Luke 24:44-53

SEVENTH SUNDAY OF EASTER READINGS
Acts 1:6-14; Psalm 68:1-10, 32-35; 1 Peter 4:12-14, 5:6-11; John 17:1-11

THEME IDEAS
Ascension Sunday reveals a power that lies within and yet beyond ordinary experience. The same power that raised Jesus from the dead and heals our bodies and our souls when we feel broken beyond repair brings gifts of the Holy Spirit that are as powerful and often fleeting as waking dreams. As Jesus is lifted up to the heavens, we are reminded to look beyond earthly power to the power of the Most High God. The immediacy of such power is

as palpable as the inability to articulate the reality of its meaning for our lives. Yet real it is.

INVITATION AND GATHERING

CENTERING WORDS (Luke 24)
The ascension of Christ forces us to contemplate powers of the Spirit that our minds cannot comprehend. But what the mind struggles to understand, the soul receives with joy.

CALL TO WORSHIP (Psalm 47, Luke 24)
Look to the heavens, people of God.
See the power of the Most High God.
Christ ascends to heaven in glory.
Shout to God with cries of joy.
Clap your hand, children of Love incarnate.
Sing praises to God, our king.

OPENING PRAYER (Acts 1, Luke 24)
God, Most High, as Christ ascended into the heavens,
    may our hearts ascend to you.
Open our eyes to the power of your Spirit,
    and open our lives to the fullness of your power,
        that we may be clothed with power on high.
Help us wait patiently for the baptism of your Spirit,
    that we may be found worthy of your great gifts.
Amen.

PROCLAMATION AND RESPONSE

PRAYER OF YEARNING (Acts 1, Ephesians 1, Luke 24)
Merciful God, we yearn for the promise
    of your glorious inheritance,
        but settle for less.
We long to see with the eyes of our hearts enlightened,
    that we might aspire to the glories of Christ above.

Teach us anew to wait for your Holy Spirit,
> that we may be clothed with power on high.
In the name of the one who ascended to heaven
> to show us the way to live here on earth, we pray.
Amen.

ASSURANCE OF PARDON *(Acts 1, Ephesians 1, Luke 24)*
Wait in patient for God's Spirit.
Wait in longing for the hope to which we are called.
God will fill us with Christ's glorious Spirit
> and clothe us with power on high.

PASSING THE PEACE OF CHRIST *(Acts 1, Luke 24)*
Brought together in the power of Christ's ascendant glory, turn and exchange signs of Christ's peace with one another this day.

INTRODUCTION TO THE WORD *(Acts 1, Luke 24)*
Prepare to receive the Spirit.
> **When will it come?**
God alone appoints the time.
> **We are ready.**
Prepare to be clothed with power from on high.
> **We are ready.**
Look and wait for Christ with expectant hearts.
> **We are ready.**

RESPONSE TO THE WORD *(Ephesians 1)*
May the God of our Lord Jesus Christ
give us a spirit of wisdom and revelation
as we come to know our heavenly creator.
> **With the eyes of our hearts enlightened,**
> **may we know the hope to which we are called**
> **and the riches of God's glorious inheritance.**
And may the immeasurable greatness of God's power,
given to those who believe, bless us each day
according to the working of God's great power.
> **Amen and amen!**

THANKSGIVING AND COMMUNION

OFFERING PRAYER (Psalm 47)
O God, for your power and might, we praise you.
For your love and mercy, we thank you.
For giving us your Spirit and your every blessing,
   we honor you with our lives and gifts.
Received from our hand the fruit of our industry,
   in ministry to a world in need of your glory.
In the name of the one who ascended to heaven,
   that we might have fullness of life here on earth,
   we pray. Amen.

SENDING FORTH

BENEDICTION (Luke 24)
Lift your eyes to the heavens.
   We lift them to the one who ascended in glory.
Trust the power of God's Holy Spirit.
   We embrace the one who clothe us with power.
Go as witnesses of the risen Lord.
   We celebrate the one who bring us eternal life.

MAY 17, 2026

Notes

May 24, 2026

Pentecost Sunday

Mary Petrina Boyd

COLOR
Red

SCRIPTURE READINGS
Acts 2:1-21; Psalm 104:24-34, 35b; 1 Corinthians 12:3b-13; John 7:37-39

THEME IDEAS
The Spirit came at Pentecost, transforming the faithful into powerful witnesses to Jesus. The message came in a variety of languages to a variety of people. First Corinthians reminds us that the gifts of the spirit are varied and each is needed for the common good. Pentecost encourages us to open our hearts to recognize God's work in a variety of people and in many circumstances. All are welcome in God's love.

INVITATION AND GATHERING

CENTERING WORDS *(Acts 2, 1 Corinthians 12)*
We wait for your Spirit, O God. Stretch our imaginations that we may see your presence in every person.

MAY 24, 2026

CALL TO WORSHIP (Acts 2)
Listen! Do you hear a sound
like the howling of a fierce wind?
Come, Holy Spirit!
Look! Can you see flames of fire?
Come, Holy Spirit!
Wait! Can you feel the power?
The Holy Spirit is here!

~or~

CALL TO WORSHIP (Psalm 104)
Sing to the Lord!
Let us sing to the Lord as long as we live!
God formed all that is: oceans and rivers,
hills and mountains.
Praise God who makes!
God created all that is: animals and birds,
fish and people.
Praise God who creates!
When God's hand opens, all are filled.
Praise God who nourishes!
Let all that we are praise God.
Praise God, now and forevermore!

OPENING PRAYER (Acts 1, 1 Corinthians 12)
Holy Spirit, power of God,
come and fill us with your strength.
May your Spirit touch each of us.
Gather us with our different gifts into one community.
Give us eyes to see your work.
May the winds of the Spirit blow away our fears,
and fill us with power.
Open our hearts,
that we may welcome everyone. Amen.

PROCLAMATION AND RESPONSE

PRAYER OF CONFESSION or PRAYER OF YEARNING (1 Corinthians 12)

> Holy One, Divine Spirt, be with us now.
> It's easy to feel like our gifts and our talents
>   aren't good enough for you.
> Help us see ourselves as part of a larger creation.
> While our gifts differ, each one is important,
>   adding something wonderful to your world.
> Our gifts come from you,
>   and they are what you want for us.
> Help us accept our own gifts.
> Enlarge our hearts,
>   so that we may recognize and welcome others,
>   each with differing gifts. Amen.

WORDS OF ASSURANCE (1 Corinthians 12)

> We are all baptized into one body.
> The Spirit blesses us all.

~or~

WORDS OF ASSURANCE (John 37)

> Rivers of living water flow out from Jesus,
>   blessing each one of us with new life.

PASSING THE PEACE OF CHRIST (1 Corinthians 12)

> The Spirit lives in each of you. We bless each other as we use our God-given talents.

PRAYER OF PREPARATION (Acts 2)

> Holy Spirit, blow away all that keeps us from you.
> Speak to us your words of power and hope.
> Open our hearts,
>   that we may hear your call for us today. Amen.

RESPONSE TO THE WORD (Acts 2)
    The good news of Jesus can't be kept in one place.
    The Spirit blew the followers of Jesus
        out into the streets and gave them language
        to reach every person.
    No one was left out.
    All were important.
    The Spirit comes today and welcomes everyone,
        even those we don't like.
    Invite the welcoming Spirit into your hearts,
        that you may see a child of God
        in everyone you meet.

THANKSGIVING AND COMMUNION

INVITATION TO THE OFFERING (1 Corinthians 12)
    God gives so many gifts to so many people. Grateful for God's abundant love, let us also bring our gifts to God.

OFFERING PRAYER (Psalm 104, 1 Corinthians 12)
    Holy one, you create all that is.
    Your breath sustains every living thing.
    In your creation,
        see your love of diversity.
    In our community,
        we celebrate the multitude of Spirit-filled gifts.
    Grateful for your care,
        we bring these gifts.
    May they spread your love to all people. Amen.

SENDING FORTH

BENEDICTION (Acts 2)
    May the flames Spirit rest upon each of you,
        blessing you with gifts of wisdom and compassion.
    May the power Spirit support you,
        opening your hearts to see God in every person.
    Go forth to proclaim the good news:
        God welcomes everyone!

Notes

May 31, 2026

Trinity Sunday

Karen Clark Ristine

COLOR
White

SCRIPTURE READINGS
Genesis 1:1–2:4a; Psalm 8; 2 Corinthians 13:11-13; Matthew 28:16-20

THEME IDEAS
The Divine is present humanity and all of creation in infinite ways—from the first breath of God at the first spark of creation, through the life, ministry, death, resurrection, and ascension of Jesus, and in the continuing aspirations of the Holy Spirit. On Trinity Sunday, we reflect on the many ways the Divine is with us and how we are called and led and nurtured to care for humanity and all of creation to the end of the age.

INVITATION AND GATHERING

CENTERING WORDS (*Matthew 28:20b, NRSV*)
"Remember, I am with you always to the end of the age."

CALL TO WORSHIP (Genesis 1, Psalm 8, Matthew 28)
In the beginning . . .
**God created mortals, and asked us to care
for all creation.**
In the fullness of time, God sent Jesus . . .
Jesus showed us how to love as God loves.
In our time, and throughout eternity . . .
**Jesus commands us to lead others
to follow in the name of the Creator,
the Christ, and the Holy Spirit. Amen.**

OPENING PRAYER (Genesis 1, Matthew 28)
Loving God, in that first spark of creativity,
 you set the cosmos in motion.
Time after time,
 your creative presence brings new life and hope.
We experience your love,
 as we see the marvels of nature.
We experience your love,
 as we study the ethics and compassion of Christ.
We experience your love
 through the ever-presence of your Holy Spirit,
  who was with you in the beginning,
   was with Christ throughout his ministry,
    and is with us to the end of the age.
For your loving presence in all your infinite ways,
 we give you thanks. Amen

PROCLAMATION AND RESPONSE

PRAYER OF YEARNING (Genesis 1, Psalm 8, Matthew 28)
Creator of us all, when we look to the heavens
 and bask in the light of the sun and the moon
  and the stars, we feel small.
Still, you call us to care for one another
 and all that your creativity set in motion.
We yearn to hear the rush of your Spirit
 sweeping over the depths of our lives,

guiding us and breathing into us vitality
to answer your call to be disciples
and to welcome others to faith in you.
Meet us in your many forms.
We yearn to respond with love. Amen.

WORDS OF ASSURANCE (Matthew 28:20b NRSV)
Jesus said: "Remember, I am with you always
to the end of the age."

PASSING THE PEACE OF CHRIST (2 Corinthians 13)
Scripture asks us to live with one another in peace, and promises us that the God of love and peace will be with us.

"The grace of the Lord Jesus Christ, the love of God,
and the communion of the Holy Spirit be with you."
And also with you.
Please greet one another with God's love, Christ's peace,
and Holy Spirit's embrace.

RESPONSE TO THE WORD (Genesis 1, Psalm 8, Matthew 28)
How majestic is your name in all the earth,
Creator of many names.
We hear and affirm your call to care for all creation,
to minister to all people,
and to trust your Divine presence,
to guide our lives this day and to the end to the age.

THANKSGIVING AND COMMUNION

OFFERING PRAYER (Genesis 1, Matthew 28, UMH hymnal membership pledge)
As we offer our prayers, our presence,
our gifts of time and resources, our service,
and our witness,
we are grateful to join in God's creative acts
to bring love and peace and hope to the world.
Amen.

THE ABINGDON WORSHIP ANNUAL 2026

SENDING FORTH

BENEDICTION
Go forth with God's Spirit, eternally present,
    even before the first instant of creation.
Go forth with Christ, present with us
    to the end of the age.
Go forth with God, joining God's creativity
    in wonder and awe. Amen.

Notes

June 7, 2026

Second Sunday after Pentecost
Proper 5

Mary Scifres
Copyright © Mary Scifres

COLOR
Green

SCRIPTURE READINGS
Genesis 12:1-9; Psalm 33:1-12; Romans 4:13-25; Matthew 9:9-13, 18-26

THEME IDEAS

The blessings God gives are blessings to be shared with others. As one who was "blessed to be a blessing" to the nations, Abraham travels to a new land with a new promise from God. This blessing, given through faith and grace rather than any particular righteousness on Abraham's part, is a blessing to be shared with every nation. Similarly, Jesus comes not to bless through righteousness, but rather through grace and faith. Blessed by God, Jesus is proclaimed God's beloved child—not through any righteousness of his own, but simply through grace and faith. Blessed by God, Jesus welcomes a tax collector to become a disciple who will share his blessings with others. Blessed by God, Jesus heals an outcast woman and a ruler's child who has a sickness unto death. The blessings are not divvied up according to righteousness, status, or identity, but rather given freely and fully as gifts of grace.

INVITATION AND GATHERING

CENTERING WORDS (Genesis 12, Matthew 9, Matthew 3:17, Mark 1:11, Luke 3:22b, 2 Peter 1:17b)
You are a blessing simply because you are God's beloved child.

CALL TO WORSHIP (Psalm 33)
Shout with joy,
for God has blessed us.
Sing with praise,
for God is here.
Worship and pray,
for God is listening.

OPENING PRAYER (Genesis 12, Psalm 33, Romans 4)
Blessed God, thank you for blessing us
in your myriad ways.
Thank you for trusting us to be your people,
to shine with your love,
and to work for your justice.
In this time of worship, guide and strengthen us,
that we may go forth to bless your world
fully and abundantly.
In your blessed name, we pray. Amen.

PROCLAMATION AND RESPONSE

PRAYER OF YEARNING (Genesis 12, Matthew 9)
Compassionate Christ, we yearn for that mysterious gift of shalom.
We long for healing and wholeness,
for peace and comfort.

But the gift all too often seems elusive, or even absent.
Touch our hearts and heal our weary souls.
Bless our wounds,
> that we may bless others in need of your love.
Soothe our fears with courage,
> that we may be strong enough to answer your call.
Raise us into new life with your miraculous grace,
> that we may be blessings of miraculous grace
>> in your world. Amen.

WORDS OF ASSURANCE *(Psalm 33, Matthew 9)*
Christ's love is faithful and true.
God's blessings are sure.
Be encouraged, dear friends,
> your faith has made you well.

PASSING THE PEACE OF CHRIST *(Genesis 12, Matthew 9)*
Blessed with God's love, let's share signs and blessings of love with others, now in this time of worship and in the week ahead.

RESPONSE TO THE WORD *(scripture references)*
God has blessed us beyond measure.
We will be blessings for God and God's world.
Holy Spirit, show us the way.
(Time for silent reflection)
Holy Spirit, show us the way.
**For we will go where you lead us,
and love as you love us.**

THANKSGIVING AND COMMUNION

INVITATION TO THE OFFERING *(Genesis 12)*
With gratitude for blessings received, we present our blessings in this time of offering. May God guide us to give generously of our time, talent, service, and treasure, that we may be blessings for the world.

OFFERING PRAYER (Genesis 12)
God of abundance and love, bless these gifts,
and bless our lives with your abundance
and your love.
In all that we have and in all that we are,
may bless and honor you
and bless and honor your beloved world. Amen.

PRAYER OF CONSECRATION (Genesis 12)
Pour out your Holy Spirit on us,
that we may be blessed beyond measure
to bless others beyond measure.
Pour our your Holy Spirit
on these gifts of bread and wine,
that they may be for us the life and love
of Christ Jesus, blessing us with strength
for the journey and with mercy and grace
for ourselves and others.
Make us one with you
through the power of your Holy Spirit,
and one with each other
Bless us to be blessings in ministry to all the world.
Amen.

SENDING FORTH

BENEDICTION (Genesis 12, Matthew 9)
God's promise is sure.
We are blessed beyond measure.
Christ's call is true.
We go forth to be blessings of love for the world.

Notes

June 14, 2026

Third Sunday after Pentecost
Proper 6 / Father's Day

Mary Scifres
Copyright © Mary Scifres

COLOR

Green

SCRIPTURE READINGS

Genesis 18:1-15; Psalm 116:1-2, 12-19; Romans 5:1-8; Matthew 9:35–10:8 (9-23)

THEME IDEAS

God's promises take a variety of forms in today's scripture readings. Abraham and Sarah receive the laughingly ridiculous promise of bearing a child in their old age. Yet the child arrives along with even more laughter—this time of joy and celebration, rather than incredulity. Paul reminds us of Christ's promises of peace, faith, and hope—all because of God's grace, rather than through any work of our own. And Jesus promises an impactful opportunity to serve the world, but this promise is tinged with dangers and toils, rejection and disappointment. God's promises are certainly not the world's promises—raising a child in one's last years of life; giving thanks for troubles because they will produce endurance, character, and hope; and

JUNE 14, 2026

answering Christ's call to serve even as sheep amongst wolves. These promises may not produce a fairytale ending, but they do produce a rich and fulfilling life.

INVITATION AND GATHERING

CENTERING WORDS (Genesis 18, Romans 5)
Hang on to God's promises, even if you have to hang on for dear life.

CALL TO WORSHIP (Genesis 18, Matthew 10)
The God of ages past and days to come is here,
inviting us to worship and praise.
The God of promises and challenges is with us,
calling us to faithful service.
The God of boundless love is with us,
making every one of God's promises possible.

OPENING PRAYER (Romans 5, Matthew 10)
Faithful One, thank you for calling us to worship
and for being present among us.
Breathe upon us with your Holy Spirit,
that we may have the courage and endurance
to trust your promises and to answer your call
with the same steadfast faithfulness and love
that you show to us. Amen.

PROCLAMATION AND RESPONSE

PRAYER OF YEARNING (Psalm 116, Genesis 18, Matthew 9-10)
We love you, O God, and we yearn to rest
in your steadfast love.
When we are restless,
calm our spirits with your Holy Spirit.
When we are lost,

guide us back to you.
When we are threatened,
    be our protective shepherd.
We can't go this alone, O God.
Be with us, and remind us that you are with us.
Help us to believe,
    even where we have not seen,
        that your loving promises may bless our lives
            and guide our steps.
In faith and trust, we pray. Amen.

WORDS OF ASSURANCE *(Genesis 18, Psalm 116)*
God listens closely to the deepest yearnings
    of our hearts.
God is listening now.
(A time of silence may follow.)
God has heard the cry of your heart,
    and will be steadfast in love and grace
        to answer our every need.

PASSING THE PEACE OF CHRIST *(Romans 5)*
Just as we have received God's peace through Christ Jesus, so now we are invited to offer God's peace to one another through the grace and love of Christ Jesus. May peace be the promise we offer to one another.

RESPONSE TO THE WORD *or* BENEDICTION
(Genesis 18, Romans 5, Matthew 9-10)
May we hear God's promises with open hearts
    and with receptive minds.
May we receive God's promises with laughter and tears.
May we trust God's promises,
    even when they seem far away.

JUNE 14, 2026

THANKSGIVING AND COMMUNION

INVITATION TO THE OFFERING (Genesis 18, Romans 5, Matthew 9-10)
>As God has promised good to us, so God invites us to offer promises of goodness to others in need. May our offerings be blessings of healing and hope to a weary world.

OFFERING PRAYER (Psalm 116, Romans 5,
1 Corinthians 13)
>Faithful and loving God, bless these gifts
>>with your faithfulness and love.
>
>Bless our lives to be faithful and loving.
>And bless our world with your promises of faith, hope, peace, and love—
>>knowing always that the greatest of these is love. Amen.

SENDING FORTH

BENEDICTION (Genesis 18, Romans 5, Matthew 10)
>As children of God's promises,
>>**we go forth to fulfill God promises to the world.**
>
>Having received peace through Christ Jesus,
>>**we go forth to bring peace to the world.**

Notes

June 21, 2026

Fourth Sunday after Pentecost
Proper 7

Mary Scifres
Copyright © Mary Scifres

COLOR
Green

SCRIPTURE READINGS
Genesis 21:8-21; Psalm 86:1-10, 16-17; Romans 6:1b-11; Matthew 10:24-39

THEME IDEAS
The plot thickens. As we delve more deeply into what it means to be children of God's promises and disciples of Christ, our journeys don't get easier. Today's scriptures indicate that the journeys grow more challenging. Having been faithful to her masters, the "chosen ones" of God, Hagar is cast aside. Having reveled in God's promises, Paul now writes of sharing in Christ's death. Even if it is only the metaphoric death to sin, death is never an easy journey. Echoing this challenge, Jesus now calls the disciples to faithful, courageous following—even if it means criticism, threats, martyrdom, rejection, division, or even carrying their own crosses toward a Roman execution.

THE ABINGDON WORSHIP ANNUAL 2026

INVITATION AND GATHERING

CENTERING WORDS *(Genesis 21, Matthew 10)*
Following the leader was simple in childhood. But following our leader, Christ Jesus, is far from simple—and often entails dangers, toils, and snares that only grace can guide us through.

CALL TO WORSHIP *(Genesis 21, Romans 6, Matthew 10)*
Through many dangers, toils, and snares,
> **we have already come.**

Through days of joy and nights of fear,
> **we've traveled this far by faith.**

Through life, through death,
> **Christ walks with us.**

We are not alone.
> **Thanks be to God!**

In this promise,
> **let's worship God together.**

(This call to worship can be preceded or be followed by the song "Amazing Grace.")

OPENING PRAYER *(Genesis 21, Psalm 86)*
Holy One, come to us now in this time of worship.
Be present our lives,
> that you may hear our cries,
> and speak to our souls.

Give us your strength,
> that we may live all the days of our lives
> in steadfast faith and hope.

JUNE 21, 2026

PROCLAMATION AND RESPONSE

PRAYER OF YEARNING (Genesis 21, Psalm 86, Matthew 10)
    Merciful God, hear our prayer.
    Hear the cries of our hearts
        and the needs of our souls.
    When we are cast aside or falling apart,
        hold us in your arms of love.
    Help us sing once again of your love
        and proclaim your strength and grace.
    Show us signs of your goodness, your presence,
        and your love, over and over again.
    Teach our hearts that we never walk alone.
        In your mercy and grace, we pray. Amen.

WORDS OF ASSURANCE (Psalm 86, Romans 6)
    God is a wonder-worker,
        and Christ is the wonder of love in our midst.
    This wondrous love is enough for every trouble we face.

INTRODUCTION TO THE WORD (Psalm 86)
    As God listens closely to us, may we listen closely for God's message to us today.

RESPONSE TO THE WORD (Genesis 21, Matthew 10)
    Christ Jesus, where you go,
        we will go.
    Where you lead,
        we will follow.
    When we fall,
        lift us up.
    When we doubt,
        be our faith.
    Where you go,
        help us faithfully and joyfully follow
        all the days of our lives.

THE ABINGDON WORSHIP ANNUAL 2026

THANKSGIVING AND COMMUNION

OFFERING PRAYER *(Genesis 21, Romans 6, Matthew 10, Father's Day)*
>Gracious God, you have blessed us as our Father,
>>as our Mother, and as our companion and friend.
>
>Christ Jesus, you have blessed as a savior and teacher,
>>and as a master and guide.
>
>We thank you for those who help us discover
>>your parenting love, your guiding companionship,
>>and your loving grace.
>
>Bless these gifts this day,
>>that others might touch your loving presence
>>in all of life. Amen.

SENDING FORTH

BENEDICTION *(Matthew 10)*
>Guided by God,
>>**we go into the world.**
>
>Led by Christ,
>>**we go with love and grace.**
>
>Strengthened by the Spirit,
>>**we go to make the world a better place.**
>>**Amen and Amen.**

Notes

June 28, 2026

Fifth Sunday after Pentecost
Proper 8

B. J. Beu
Copyright © B. J. Beu

COLOR

Green

SCRIPTURE READINGS

Genesis 22:1-14; Psalm 13; Romans 6:12-23; Matthew 10:40-42

THEME IDEAS

No matter how hard we try, we cannot avoid the pain and trials of life. The psalmist speaks of the trials of faith, as we seek God's comfort and protection. Genesis highlights the trials of conflicting loyalties, as we struggle to follow God with personal integrity and with loyalty to those we love. Romans illustrates the trials of earthly passions and sinful temptations, even as we aspire to walk with Christ. Yet, amid our pain and fears of abandonment, God is there to rescue us and lead us safely home.

JUNE 28, 2026

INVITATION AND GATHERING

CENTERING WORDS *(Matthew 10)*
In Christ Jesus, all are welcome here. Welcome, people of God!

CALL TO WORSHIP *(Genesis 22, Psalm 13)*
When the Lord seems far away,
may we place our faith in God.
When God's face is hidden from us,
may we put our trust in God's steadfast love.
When our souls bear the pain of earthly trials,
may we seek God's strength, lest we break.
Let us place our trust in God's goodness and mercy.
Our hearts rejoice in God's salvation.

OPENING PRAYER *(Psalm 13, Matthew 10)*
God of pain and suffering, embrace us in our need.
As we enter this house of worship,
you know our deepest needs,
and you help us embrace our sincerest hopes.
Live in us this day, and quicken our spirits,
that we may rise above the storms
that threaten to overcome us.
We ask this the name of the one who came
to bring us abundant life. Amen.

PROCLAMATION AND RESPONSE

PRAYER OF YEARNING *(Genesis 22, Psalm 13)*
Merciful God, as we travel the difficult paths of life,
it is easy to forget that you are always there,
even when we feel abandoned and alone.
Help us move beyond our anguish, Holy One,
that we might set aside our self-absorption,
even as we seek your salvation.

Lead us in the ways of life,
> for we yearn to feel your presence
> amid our deepest despair.
Elevate our hearts and minds above our fear and doubt,
> that we may embrace your grace and mercy. Amen.

ASSURANCE OF PARDON (Romans 6)

Even amid seasons of doubt and grief,
> God offers us eternal life through the love
> of Christ Jesus, our Lord.

PASSING THE PEACE OF CHRIST (Matthew 10)

During the storms of life, let us show our gratitude for our source of strength and courage by sharing the peace of Christ with one another.

RESPONSE TO THE WORD (Psalm 13)

Even when we are afraid,
> let us sing to the Lord.
> **We will sing to the Lord with joy in our hearts.**
Even when God seems far away,
> let us shout to the Lord.
> **We will shout to the Lord with hope in our souls.**
Even when we find ourselves far from home,
> let us walk with the Lord with faith.
> **We will walk with the Lord all the way home.**

THANKSGIVING AND COMMUNION

OFFERING PRAYER (Genesis 22)

Bountiful God, when we come to you with nothing,
> you provide us with the offering.
When life's demands threaten to overwhelm us,
> you spare us the deadly cost.
In tribute and thanks for your manifold blessings,
> we offer you what we have
> > in certain hope of your abiding love. Amen.

JUNE 28, 2026

SENDING FORTH

BENEDICTION *(Genesis 22, Psalm 13, Romans 6)*
Even when the Lord seems far away
and our faith is sorely tested,
> **we will put our trust in God's steadfast love.**

Even when our souls bear the pain of earthly trials
and our strengths seems to slip away,
> **we will trust God's goodness and mercy.**

Even when we question God's presence in our lives
and our hearts feel heavy with fear,
> **we go forth as those sanctified with eternal life.**

Go with God.

Notes

July 5, 2026

Sixth Sunday after Pentecost
Proper 9

Kirsten Linford

COLOR

Green

SCRIPTURE READINGS

Genesis 24:34-38, 42-49, 58-67; Psalm 45:10-17; Romans 7:15-25a; Matthew 11:16-19, 25-30

THEME IDEAS

These are not necessarily easy texts to deal with. Though not overtly violent or oppressive, they point to some of the more subtly problematic aspects of womanhood in the Bible. In Genesis 24 and Psalm 45, blessings are laid upon the marriages of two different women (one specific and named, the other more general and unnamed). Those blessings relate specifically to the expectation that they will have children. While we don't know how that will work out for the princess in the psalm, those who have read ahead will know that Rebekah will endure two decades of infertility before finally giving birth to twin sons. Rebekah will ultimately show herself to be more than either of those tropes when she schemes with Jacob to manipulate Esau out of his birthright. But what some might see as devious others would interpret as canny and cunning—a woman who finds and creates her own agency. Without her actions, would Jacob have become a leader of his people? Would we judge her actions as harshly if done by a man? Perhaps the text leads us to embrace the complexity of biblical narratives. How would such complexity serve us in reading the Romans text? Could we expand beyond the mind vs. the flesh dichotomy?

INVITATION AND GATHERING

CENTERING WORDS (*Gensis 24, Psalm 45*)
'May you, our sister, become thousands of myriads; may your offspring gain possession of the gates of their foes' .... Hear, O daughter, consider and incline your ear .... In the place of ancestors you ... shall have sons; you will make them princes in all the earth. I will cause your name to be celebrated in all generations; therefore the peoples will praise you for ever and ever.

CALL TO WORSHIP (*Genesis 24*)
The Lord has greatly blessed us,
    with all that we need and more.
God has done miracles in our lives
    beyond what we could ask,
or comprehend
    or even hope for.
The Holy One has made us
    thousands of myriads—
not just one thing,
    but multitudes.
Let us come now,
    again ...
always ...
    to offer our praise to the Creator of all.

OPENING PRAYER *(Genesis 24, Psalm 45)*
God of all Life, you take what feels complicated
    and make it simple.
You take what seems simple
    and show us the complex.
You remind us that we are
    more than we think we are,
        more than we believe we can be,
            and all that you have made us
                and called us to become.
Come, God, and lead us forward
    with joy and gladness.
Come, God, and help us see past
    the expectations and assumptions
        into the world you long for us to create
            with mercy and space, justice and grace,
                for us all. Amen.

PROCLAMATION AND RESPONSE

PRAYER OF YEARNING *(Genesis 24, Psalm 45)*
God of us all,
    we incline our ears to you now,
        listening, again,
            for the sound of your voice.
We do not always remember to listen, O God.
We do not always remember to hear
    when you speak into our hearts.
We do not always remember to look
    deeper than the surface.
We do not always seek your guidance
    or follow it.
But we remember now,
    and we long to listen now—
        to hear and to see,
        to seek and to follow.

JULY 5, 2026

Turn us away from all that is just noise
    and back to the sound of your soul.
To your heart beating for us always. Amen.

WORDS OF ASSURANCE (Psalm 45)
God speaks into our hearts words of love
    and of grace.
With joy and gladness does our Creator lead us
    into life.
The Holy One makes each of our names
    a celebration in all generations
    and in this moment too.
For God has made us whole again,
    and again.

PASSING THE PEACE OF CHRIST (Matthew 11:28)
Christ says to us, "Come to me, all you that are weary and weighed down, and I will give you rest." Christ gives us rest and peace. Let us share it with one another.

PRAYER OF PREPARATION (Psalm 19)
May the words of my mouth . . .
    and the meditations of our hearts be acceptable
    in your sight, O Lord, our strength
    and our redeemer. Amen.

RESPONSE TO THE WORD (Romans 7)
Let us delight in the law of God
    in our inmost selves—
        with our minds and with our hearts,
        with our bodies and with our souls.
    All parts joined together
        in the grace of God. Amen.

THANKSGIVING AND COMMUNION

INVITATION TO THE OFFERING (Genesis 24, Matthew 11)
Christ invites us to live and serve with him—letting his burden lighten our own. He multiplies the gifts we share—making thousands of myriads of love and of blessing.

OFFERING PRAYER (Genesis 24, Psalm 45)
Gracious God, you have made our lives more
    than we ever dreamed,
        offering blessings beyond our greatest imaginings,
            multitudes of mercy, great gifts of grace.
From this bounty, we offer ourselves and our lives—
    our time, talents, and treasures—
        with joy and gladness,
            for now and for always. Amen.

SENDING FORTH

BENEDICTION (2 Kings 2)
People of God, may you become thousands of myriads:
Love incarnate. Grace in every moment.
Go and live in peace, this day and all days. Amen.

JULY 5, 2026

Notes

July 12, 2026

Seventh Sunday after Pentecost
Proper 10

Mary Scifres
Copyright © Mary Scifres

COLOR

Green

SCRIPTURE READINGS

Genesis 25:19-34; Psalm 119:105-112; Romans 8:1-11; Matthew 13:1-9, 18-23

THEME IDEAS

Even when we are blessed, struggles are a fact of life. The struggle within Rebekah's womb becomes a struggle between her children, not just in childhood, but throughout their adult lives. Today, we move from the Abraham-Isaac cycle, to the Jacob-Esau cycle—a cycle of great division and despair for both men. Their story points to a reality we all face, even when we are striving to live in the Spirit of God's love and peace, for many challenges become struggles, sometimes of our own making and sometimes imposed upon us. In the struggle, God's word and Spirit offer guidance, but we may miss it as Esau did, and find ourselves caught in the weeds.

JULY 12, 2026

INVITATION AND GATHERING

CENTERING WORDS *(Psalm 119, Matthew 13)*
God's word is the lamp we need in the darkness, the guidance we need on wayward paths, and the hope we need when death and despair come calling.

CALL TO WORSHIP *(Genesis 25, Matthew 13)*
Come, whether weary or rejoicing.
All are welcome here.
Come, whether at peace or in the midst of a struggle.
All are welcome here.
Come, whether growing or wilting.
All are welcome here.

OPENING PRAYER *(Genesis 25, Psalm 119, Matthew 13)*
God of new beginnings and ancient stories,
    help us see ourselves in your stories,
        in your promises, and in your garden.
Light our way with your word today,
    and guide us with your Spirit of love. Amen.

PROCLAMATION AND RESPONSE

PRAYER OF YEARNING *(Genesis 25, Romans 8, Matthew 13)*
Holy God, we want to be your perfect children.
But like Jacob and Esau before us,
    we are far from perfect.
In our yearning, we're as likely to settle for second best
    or to reach for things that seem so right
        but ultimately draw us further away from you.
Help us choose the better portion.
Give us the courage to grow as disciples in your word,
    even when it seems hard.

And when the thorns and weeds begin choking us,
> resuscitate us with your grace,
> revive us with your love,
> and reclaim us as your children,
>> imperfect though we may be.
In grateful hope, we pray. Amen.

WORDS OF ASSURANCE (Romans 8, Matthew 13)
> The Spirit of Christ is strong enough
>> for even the weariest of spirits.
> Rest in Christ's Spirit, and you will find comfort.
> Trust in Christ's Spirit, and growth will begin anew.

PASSING THE PEACE OF CHRIST (Genesis 25)
> Setting aside past hurts, let us offer signs of peace and love to friends and family both near and far.

INTRODUCTION TO THE WORD (Psalm 119)
> God's word is a lamp before our feet, a light to open our minds, and grace to soothe our souls. May God's word bless and guide us this day.

RESPONSE TO THE WORD (Genesis 25, Romans 8)
> Peace of Christ Jesus, holy peace.
> **Peace for our divisions, holy peace.**
> Peace of God's Spirit, holy peace.
> **Peace for our striving, holy peace.**
> Peace of God's power, holy peace.
> **Peace for our world, holy peace.**
> May these be ours this day.
> **Amen.**

THANKSGIVING AND COMMUNION

OFFERING PRAYER (Genesis 25)
> Creator God, you have created us for your purposes and blessed us to accomplish your promises.

JULY 12, 2026

May the gifts and lives we offer to you
 serve your purposes and your promises,
  and may we be instruments of peace and love
   in your world each day. Amen.

SENDING FORTH

BENEDICTION (*Genesis 25, Romans 8*)
As children of God's promises,
 we will bring God's promised love the world.
As recipients of Christ's peace,
 we will bring Christ's peace to the world.
Blessed by the Holy Spirit,
 we will bless everyone we meet.

(For more ideas related to Matthew 13, consult The Abingdon Worship Annual 2023 *and* 2020, *or visit https://www.creative-worshipmadeeasy.com/)*

Notes

July 19, 2026

Eighth Sunday after Pentecost
Proper 11

Anna Crews Camphouse

COLOR
Green

SCRIPTURE READINGS
Genesis 28:10-19a; Psalm 139:1-12, 23-24; Romans 8:12-25; Matthew 13:24-30, 36-43

THEME IDEAS
Genesis reminds us that God keeps promises from generation to generation. The psalmist proclaims God knows everything about us, even the things we would rather hide. Matthew asserts there are always seeds of holy goodness within us that God wants to harvest in God's field of heavenly dreaming. The Romans text knows that being human comes with joys and sufferings. God celebrates our successes and grieves with us in our sufferings. Even in our greatest frustrations, we can trust that God is with us, empowering us with hope, trust, and faith. The Spirit brings freedom from suffering and strength in times of great need, working all things together for good. The seeds of God's kin-dom grow and reproduce throughout the ages,

asking us to reconsider our role as God's beloved children who are parts of the holy garden of life.

INVITATION AND GATHERING

CENTERING WORDS (Genesis 28, Romans 8, Matthew 13)
> Breathe in and consider what God has done throughout the generations. Breathe out and know that God abides with us in our sufferings and frustrations. Breathe in and dream of what God can do. Breathe out in hope and gratitude for what God will do in worship today.

CALL TO WORSHIP (Genesis 28, Psalm 139)
> God knows us better than we know ourselves.
>> **Even in the darkest places, the light of God's love is there.**
>
> There is nowhere we can flee from God's presence.
>> **In the heavens and in the depths, the Holy One abides with us.**
>
> We are God's children, serving the Lord from generation to generation.
>> **God is the one who keeps promises and who provides for us wherever we go.**
>
> How awesome is this place!
>> **This is God's house and the gateway to the heavens.**

OPENING PRAYER (Genesis 28)
> Source of dreams, we seek to find deep renewal
>> in our faithful worship and reflection.
>
> Sleeping humans are all around us,
>> plugged into mindless activities
>>> like scrolling, playing games,
>>>> or watching for the trend of the day,
>>>>> rather than the deep hope for our souls.

Our friends often sleepwalk through the day,
    looking for ways to stay isolated,
        rather than connected,
            actively working to avoid conflict
                and relationship building.
We seek to remember our connection with you,
    as generations before us and generations to come.
Come into this space and enliven our hearts,
    that we may feel your creative spirit guiding us
        into the next steps of where we should go
            to bring people into a genuine community.
Amen.

PROCLAMATION AND RESPONSE

PRAYER OF YEARNING (Romans 8, Matthew 13)
Abba God, as our heavenly parent,
    you have given us your words of direction
        to teach us how to live by eternal truths.
Still, we struggle with the fleshly desires
    that slow our living into our most abundant lives.
We ache for the breath of your compassion
    to restore us to spiritual health.
Assist us to live in freedom instead of fear.
Imbue our minds with deep compassion,
    that we may find fulfillment
        in caring for the world around us.
Help us deal with the weeds of distrust, greed,
    anger, lust, isolation, jealousy, and egoism
        that manifest as abuses and the denigration
            of others.
May we be increasingly strengthened as your children
    and shine like the sun in our hurting world. Amen.

JULY 19, 2026

WORDS OF ASSURANCE *(Genesis 28, Psalm 139, Romans 8)*
God searches and knows you.
God is familiar with all your ways.
God loves you as a precious child,
   making you co-heirs of glory
   and the multi-generational promises
   that free us from frustration and fill us with hope.
Peace and hope are yours in the name of Christ. Amen.

RESPONSE TO THE WORD *(Matthew 13)*
May the seed of your goodness and grace
   grow mightily through our lives.
May the Planter fulfill through our prayerful service
   the ripe harvest of the light of divine love.
Striving toward the Son, we commit the fruitful wheat
   of our discipleship to you.

THANKSGIVING AND COMMUNION

OFFERING PRAYER *(Genesis 28, Matthew 13)*
Holy Harvester, you have been planting seeds
   of blessing and provision for thousands of years.
In gratitude for all You have done,
   we give you thanks and praise.
For the work you have called us
   to accomplish in this season,
      we give our prayers, presence, gifts, service,
         and witness.
For the harvest yet to come,
   we pray for your direction and protection,
     that all we contribute may bring forth
       your fruitful bounty
         in the field of your heavenly dream.
Amen.

SENDING FORTH

BENEDICTION (Matthew 13)
   Grow strong, taking in the living waters of love.
   Grow deeply, being grounded and rooted in faith.
   Grow to new heights of love and mercy,
      moving always toward the mercy, justice, and truth
      of God's dream.
   Go from this place in a growth mindset,
      lighting up the world with the illuminating grace
      of God's presence. Amen.

Notes

July 26, 2026

Ninth Sunday after Pentecost
Proper 12

Mary Scifres
Copyright © Mary Scifres

COLOR

Green

SCRIPTURE READINGS

Genesis 29:15-28; Psalm 105:1-11, 45b; Romans 8:26-39; Matthew 13:31-33, 44-52

THEME IDEAS

The mysterious way in which God acts in and through us flows as a theme through each of today's scripture readings. Paul promises that nothing can separate us from God's love, but there are certainly plenty of things that separate us from one another and from living fully into God's promises. Jacob will somehow continue to live his grandfather Abraham's promise to be the father of great nations, but must first endure a trickster uncle and then spend the rest of his life managing two sister-wives and the many children they will bear for him. Jesus speaks cryptically and poetically about the kingdom of heaven, leaving us with more questions than answers, but still inspiring us to search for meaning and purpose as followers of God.

Accepting the mysteries of God is perhaps as much a part of our faithfulness as is accepting our call to discipleship.

INVITATION AND GATHERING

CENTERING WORDS (Romans 8)
The same Spirit that formed the church on Pentecost forms our lives each day. Strengthening us in our weakness, the Spirit reminds us that nothing can separate us from the love of God that is ours in Christ Jesus.

CALL TO WORSHIP (Psalm 105 Romans 8)
Give thanks to God, for God is good.
God's goodness and mercy are sure.
Sing to the Spirit, for the Spirit is here.
The Spirit knows the ache for connection deep within us.
Praise Christ Jesus, who loves us
with a love that is boundless and true.
Give thanks to God, and sing God's praise,
as we worship together this day.

OPENING PRAYER (Romans 8, Matthew 13)
Loving God, thank you for calling us to worship today.
Thank you for sending your Spirit to speak
to and for our spirits,
strengthening our weary souls
and empowering us to live and serve.
Send your Spirit into our worship today,
that we may fully sense your presence
and embrace your mysterious wisdom.
In your holy name, we pray. Amen.

JULY 26, 2026

PROCLAMATION AND RESPONSE

PRAYER OF YEARNING (Genesis 29, Romans 8, Matthew 13)
    God of mystery and majesty,
        we want to understand your ways,
        but we seldom can.
    Help us accept the unfathomable truth of your love.
    Help us embrace the mystery of your wisdom.
    Grant us patience when your promises seem delayed,
        and grant us perseverance when we are tempted
        to turn away in despair.
    Most of all, reveal your love to us,
        that we may truly trust this truth—
            that nothing can separate us from your love,
            your mercy, and your grace.
    In hope and faith, we pray. Amen.

WORDS OF ASSURANCE (Romans 8)
    My friends, these words are faithful and true,
        even when we aren't really sure: Nothing—
    absolutely nothing in all of creation,
    in all of our histories, in all of our actions,
    and in all of our world—
        can separate us from God's love in Christ Jesus
        our Lord.

PASSING THE PEACE OF CHRIST (Romans 8)
    As we are loved beyond our wildest imaginations by the God who formed us from dust, may we share this mysterious abundant love with one another, as we share signs of peace this day.

RESPONSE TO THE WORD (Genesis 29, Psalm 105, Romans 8)
    Remembering God's covenant,
    we are invited to trust God's love.

God's love knows no bounds,
and nothing can stop it.
The Spirit is with us, intertwined with our souls
and present in our world.
The Spirit's power is mighty,
and nothing can stop it.
Christ's grace is real, amazing and abundant.
In this grace, we are promised love everlasting,
love that sticks with us for better or worse.
Thanks be to God for these amazing gifts!

THANKSGIVING AND COMMUNION

OFFERING PRAYER *(Genesis 29, Romans 8)*
Miraculous God, bless these gifts
with your miraculous love.
Bless our offerings with the mystery of an abundance
that expands and grows,
so that all may know the truth of your love—
a love that cannot be stopped
no matter what.
Bless us to bring forth your miraculous love
in all that we say and do. Amen.

SENDING FORTH

BENEDICTION *(Romans 8, Matthew 13)*
Beloved ones, go now to love.
We will grow God's realm.
Beloved of God, go to proclaim Christ's grace.
We will be vessels of mercy and live in the Spirit.

JULY 26, 2026

Notes

August 2, 2026

Tenth Sunday after Pentecost
Proper 13

Michael Beu
Copyright © Michael Beu

COLOR

Green

SCRIPTURE READINGS

Genesis 32:22-31; Psalm 17:1-7, 15; Romans 9:1-5; Matthew 14:13-21

THEME IDEAS

Doubt, faith, and blessing are interwoven in today's scripture readings. Jacob doubts he can cross Esau's land without being attacked, so he sends his family and flocks ahead. When confronted by an angel, Jacob is not shamed by his earlier lack of faith but demands to be blessed. Paul has no doubt that God has called him to preach to the Gentiles, yet this does not annul the blessings God has bestowed upon Israel. And while Jesus' disciples want to send the crowds away for food, Jesus knows that they themselves could bless the hungry followers with food if they had sufficient faith. Even in our doubts, blessings are to be had by those who have faith in the One who blesses us. An additional theme is seeing God face to face. Jacob sees God face to face as he struggles with the angel. The psalmist is confident in seeing God's face in righteousness.

INVITATION AND GATHERING

CENTERING WORDS (Matthew 14)
God's love and grace welcome us here. Christ's bounty feeds us at his table.

CALL TO WORSHIP (Matthew 14)
My people are hungry.
There are too many to feed.
Give them something to eat.
We have only five loaves and two fish.
You have everything you need.
It would take a miracle.
With God, all things are possible.
In Christ, new hope has dawned.

OPENING PRAYER (Genesis 32)
Even when our faith falters, O Lord,
we will not let you go.
Even though we are battered and bruised, O God,
we will not let you go.
Even when our bellies are empty,
we know your presence will satisfy us.
We need your blessing, O God,
and we will not let you go. Amen.

PROCLAMATION AND RESPONSE

PRAYER OF YEARNING (Genesis 32, Matthew 14)
God of mystery and power, you call us home
amid our fear and doubt.
When we are hungry and weary,
we yearn to be filled and revived.

When our faith wavers,
> we long to forsake our clever schemes
>> and find shelter in your ways.
When faced with those in need,
> we dream of doing the impossible
>> for you are with us and work through us.
Stay with us when we have need of you, O God,
> and bless us in our struggles,
>> that we might be a blessing for others. Amen.

WORDS OF ASSURANCE (Psalm 17, Matthew 14)
Awaken to the good news of God's love:
In Christ, we find strength for the journey
and are fed by God's gracious hand.

PASSING THE PEACE OF CHRIST (Psalm 17)
As we strive to keep our feet on the paths of peace, we look to our sisters and brothers in Christ for encouragement and hope for the journey. Let us turn and draw strength from one another as we share signs of Christ's peace.

RESPONSE TO THE WORD (Genesis 32, Psalm 17, Matthew 14)
Compassionate One, feed us with the wisdom
> of your enduring word,
>> even as you feed us at your table of grace.
Touch our minds with understanding,
> that we may sense your presence
>> in the struggles and wounds of life. Amen.

THANKSGIVING AND COMMUNION

INVITATION TO THE OFFERING (Matthew 14)
Faced with a hungry crowd and only five loaves and two fish, Jesus fed the multitude until all were satisfied. Faced with a hungry world, God invites us to show our faith and offer our gifts, that all might be satisfied.

OFFERING PRAYER (Matthew 14)
   Source of Compassion, all you have given us is yours.
   May our gifts become loaves and fish
      for those who hunger.
   May our offerings become love and light
      for those who feel lost and afraid.
   Help us share our abundance with those in want,
      that the world may be fed
         and made whole again. Amen.

INVITATION TO COMMUNION (Matthew 14)
   God of hopes and dreams,
      we are empty and long to be filled;
      we are hungry and long to be fed;
      we are lost and long to be found.
   Gather us in your love,
      and pick up the pieces of our lives,
         that nothing may be lost.
   Call us anew to eat our fill at Christ's table
      of the bread of life, the hope of the ages. Amen.

SENDING FORTH

BENEDICTION (Genesis 32, Matthew 14)
   Go with the One who brings us through the wilderness
   into a land flowing with milk and honey.
      We go with the blessings of God,
      who greets us face to face.
   Go with the One who heals our wounds
   and makes us whole.
      We go with the blessings of God,
      who bathes us in the power of the Holy Spirit.

Notes

August 9, 2026

Eleventh Sunday after Pentecost
Proper 14

Lisa Ann Moss Degrenia

COLOR
Green

SCRIPTURE READINGS
Genesis 37:1-4, 12-28; Psalm 105:1-6, 16-22, 45b; Romans 10:5-15; Matthew 14:22-33

THEME IDEAS

In Matthew 14:22-33, the disciples are overwhelmed with exhaustion after far too many hours battling the storm. They are literally being tormented by the waves. Even though many are seasoned fishermen, they realize their skills will not save them from the life-threatening situation. In the early morning hours, in the deep darkness, with the winds roaring and the waves crashing, Jesus comes straight for them. They mistake him for a spirit of death, but soon experience him as the powerful, rescuing, Son of God.

INVITATION AND GATHERING

CENTERING WORDS *(Matthew 14)*
If you find yourself in raging waters, deep waters, do not fear. Look . . . trust . . . your rescue is near.

CALL TO WORSHIP *(Matthew 14)*
Christ comes for us in sunshine and in the dead of night.
Welcome the presence of Christ.
We welcome you, O Christ!
Blessed be your name!
Christ reaches out to us in the stillness of peace
and in the rage of the storm.
Nothing overwhelms our Savior.
Nothing overcomes.
Our hope and trust are in you!
Blessed be your name!

OPENING PRAYER *(Matthew 14)*
Merciful Christ, fill us with your faith and courage,
    that we may never be overwhelmed by great needs,
        but rather with your great grace,
           your great strength,
           your great compassion,
           your great presence,
           your great hope.
Fulfill your greatness in us and through us
    for the honor and glory of your name,
    for the saving of lives,
    for the redemption of four world. Amen.

PROCLAMATION AND RESPONSE

PRAYER OF YEARNING *(Matthew 14)*
Jesus, there are times we test you,
    asking you to prove yourself.

We mistrust your truth.
We long for assurance.
Steady us against the howls of suspicion and fear.

Jesus, there are times when we lose sight of you.
The waves rise too high.
The wind cries too loud.
The storm distracts us, dragging us under.
We're in over our heads.
Reach out. Reach out now, with your saving embrace.

Jesus, there are times we risk too little.
We cling to the tiny ship of what we see and know.
Lead us into courage and action.
Help us long for the great adventure of you
    and your saving work.

I invite you to offer your own prayers, silently or aloud.
(Allow time for prayer.)

WORDS OF ASSURANCE *(Matthew 14)*

When the unexpected comes;
    when the unthinkable overwhelms;
    when our choices lead to despair;
    remember the words of Jesus,
    "Take heart, I AM, do not be afraid."
Remember the grace of Jesus, reaching out,
    raising us up.
Remember the power of Jesus,
    the Son of the One, True, Living God.

PASSING THE PEACE OF CHRIST *(Matthew 14)*

Jesus extends the hand of peace and saving love. In this same spirit, let us share signs of Christ's peace and love with one another.

RESPONSE TO THE WORD *(Matthew 14)*
In the deep of night, Jesus comes.
Thanks be to God!
In the chaos and fear, Jesus comes.
Thanks be to God!
In the grip of death, Jesus comes.
Thanks be to God!

LITANY *(Matthew 14)*
Jesus, we see you calming storms,
storm-tossed seas and stormy lives.
Extend your power and grace again,
upon us and all in need.
Extend peace and healing over bodies and spirits
overwhelmed by crashing waves of circumstance.
Jesus, make peace.
(Moment of silence.)
Extend peace and perspective over minds and hearts
adrift in confusion or drowning in fear.
Jesus, make peace.
(Moment of silence.)
Extend peace and hope over people, families,
and communities swamped by danger, injustice,
and loss.
Jesus, make peace.
(Moment of silence.)
I invite you to offer your own prayers, silently or aloud.
(Allow time for praying.)
Jesus, truly you are the Son of God.
You are strong to save.
Help us to live the prayer you taught us.
(Conclude with the Lord's Prayer.)

THANKSGIVING AND COMMUNION

OFFERING PRAYER *(Matthew 14)*
    Generous One, you reach down to raise us
        from fear and death.
    You reach down so that we may reach out
        with your hope and help.
    Bless, accept, and multiply this offering,
        so many may know you, your saving power,
        and your saving love. Amen.

SENDING FORTH

BENEDICTION *(Matthew 14)*
    Beloved of God, go now in peace to make peace.
    Go, reaching out in love, extending the hand of grace
        and life to those in need.
    Go with the blessing and power of Almighty God—
        Father, Son, Spirit. Amen.

Notes

August 16, 2026

Twelfth Sunday after Pentecost
Proper 15

B. J. Beu
Copyright © B. J. Beu

COLOR
Green

SCRIPTURE READINGS
Genesis 45:1-15; Psalm 133; Romans 11:1-2a, 29-32; Matthew 15:(10-20) 21-28

THEME IDEAS
What unites us is far greater than what divides us. Joseph forgives his brothers for selling him into slavery, for God used this terrible act to save Israelites and Egyptians alike from famine. The psalmist celebrates when kindred live together in unity. Paul asks rhetorically if God has rejected the Hebrew people by offering salvation to the Gentiles, and answers no. Jesus initially refuses to help a Canaanite woman's daughter until she presses her case. Then Jesus joyfully heals the daughter, marveling at the mother's faith. We are all bound together in the unconditional love of God.

INVITATION AND GATHERING

CENTERING WORDS *(Genesis 47, Psalm 133, Matthew 15)*
God's grace and presence lie hidden in moments of abandonment and loss. The time we feel most alone is the time we are most closely held.

CALL TO WORSHIP *(Genesis 45, Psalm 133, Romans 11, Matthew 15)*
When hatred and division separate us,
God's love binds us together.
When quarrels estrange us,
Christ's grace brings reconciliation.
When we feel excluded and left out,
The Spirit's peace eases our pain.
Come! Let us worship the One who makes us one.

OPENING PRAYER *(Genesis 45, Psalm 133, Romans 11, Matthew 15)*
Eternal God, heal the wounds that block our unity
as your beloved children.
Ease the hurts and betrays the block us
from embracing the balm of your forgiveness.
Cast out the fears that prevent us from seeking
your peace and reconciliation.
Even when our hearts are pierced with anguish,
send us friends who will bring us solace,
through your loving Spirit. Amen.

PROCLAMATION AND RESPONSE

PRAYER OF YEARNING *(Genesis 45, Psalm 133, Matthew 15)*
Merciful God, free us from the desire for retribution
towards those who have wronged us.
And fill us mercy and compassion
for those who trigger deep-seated prejudices
against those who offend us.

Open our hearts, O God,
    to those who seem different and strange.
For we long to know the joy of living in peace,
    and the hope of living in harmony,
        with those we would rather live without. Amen.

ASSURANCE OF PARDON (Romans 11)
The gifts and the calling of God are irrevocable.
Rejoice in the knowledge of God's saving love.

RESPONSE TO THE WORD (Genesis 45, Psalm 133, Romans 11, Matthew 15)
Even amid apparent tragedy,
    God's love gathers up the fragments of our lives.
Even amid apparent rejection,
    God's faithfulness rescues us from despair.
Even when we feel abandoned and alone,
    God calls us to find strength for the journey.
Even amid strife,
    God calls us to look beyond our differences.
Let us live together in unity.

THANKSGIVING AND COMMUNION

OFFERING PRAYER (Genesis 22)
Faithful One, when hunger threatens our world,
    you bless us with dreams
        that we can save the children of our day.
Bless this offering,
    that your dreams for a world without want
        may bless the lives of your children.
Transform these gifts into vessels of grace
    that have the power to make all people one.
In your holy name, we pray. Amen.

THE ABINGDON WORSHIP ANNUAL 2026

SENDING FORTH

BENEDICTION (Genesis 22, Romans 6)
The God of dreams has brought us together.
The God of dreams sends us forth as one.
The God of love has knit us together in unity.
The God of love heals our divisions.
The God of hope sends us forth together.
The God of peace brings peace to our world.

Notes

August 23, 2026

Thirteenth Sunday after Pentecost
Proper 16

B. J. Beu
Copyright © B. J. Beu

COLOR
Green

SCRIPTURE READINGS
Exodus 1:8–2:10; Psalm 124; Romans 12:1-8; Matthew 16:13-20

THEME IDEAS

It takes a village to build the realm of God. Each person has a role to play. It took a village of women (the midwives Shiphrah and Puah, Moses' mother and sister, and the daughter of Pharaoh) to birth, protect, and raise Moses—the leader who would lead the Hebrew people from slavery and oppression. It took Peter and the disciples to proclaim the good news after Jesus' death. It took people with many and diverse spiritual gifts to fill the church with the talents it needed to thrive. Truly, it takes a village to build the realm of God.

INVITATION AND GATHERING

CENTERING WORDS *(Exodus 1–2, Psalm 124, Matthew 16)*
It takes a village to build the realm of God. It takes each of us to play our role and work together to build the kingdom.

CALL TO WORSHIP *(Exodus 1–2)*
Amid the forces of death and destruction,
it takes a village to save us.
Amid the rivers that would carry us out to sea,
it takes willing souls to pull us from the water.
Amid the fear and hatred in our world,
it takes ordinary people to reveal God's mercy.
Come, let us worship.

OPENING PRAYER *(Romans 12)*
Gracious God, we present our very lives
as holy and living sacrifices to your purposes.
During this time of worship,
we seek the renewal of our minds
and the strengthening of our spirits.
Show us your will,
that we may know what is good, acceptable,
and perfect in your sight. Amen.

PROCLAMATION AND RESPONSE

PRAYER OF YEARNING *(Exodus 1–2)*
Merciful God, wash away the injuries
we have inflicted upon one another.
We long to replace our bitterness in word and deed
with acts of grace and mercy.
We yearn to replace our willful neglect of others
with acts of support and grace.

We desire to walk in your path of joy and compassion,
   that we may bathe in the waters
      of your healing love. Amen.

WORDS OF ASSURANCE (Psalm 124)
Thanks be to God who rescues us from our foes.
Thanks be to Christ who saves us from forces
   that would be our undoing.
In God's loving Spirit, we are set free
   and made whole again.

PASSING THE PEACE (Romans 12, Matthew 16)
When we recognize Christ for who he really is, we find the peace and security to see ourselves for who we really are. Let us share this peace with one another as we pass the peace of Christ this day.

RESPONSE TO THE WORD (Exodus 1–2, Romans 12)
God of mercy and compassion, hear our prayer.
As your men of old heeded the cries
   of suffering and injustice in their day,
      help us heed the cries of suffering and injustice
         in our world today.
As you moved the hearts of women of old,
   to save those in peril from the wicked,
      move our hearts to save the weak
         who cannot help themselves today.
Bind us together into a village of love and support,
   that we might saves your children
      from death and destruction. Amen.

THANKSGIVING AND COMMUNION

INVITATION TO THE OFFERING (Exodus 1–2, Romans 12, Matthew 16)
God's light shines through giving hearts and generous spirits. Christ's voice speaks through acts of healing in our

world. In our sharing, let us bring the light and love of
God's kingdom to a world in need.

OFFERING PRAYER *(Exodus 1–2, Romans 12)*
Loving God, accept our gifts
    as signs of our commitment
        to build your realm in our midst.
Accept our very lives
    as pledges of our commitment
        to pursue what is good, acceptable, and perfect
           in your sight.
May these gifts become resources
    to draw the endangered from the waters of death,
        through Jesus Christ, our Lord. Amen.

SENDING FORTH

BENEDICTION *(Exodus 1–2, Mark 16)*
Blessed are you who resist the forces
    of death and destruction.
Blessed are you who heed the cries of the weak
    and the helpless.
Blessed are you who build the kingdom of God
    with your love and compassion.
Blessed are you who commit yourselves
    to do what is right and honorable and true.

AUGUST 23, 2026

Notes

THE ABINGDON WORSHIP ANNUAL 2026

August 30, 2026

Fourteenth Sunday after Pentecost
Proper 17

Kirsten Linford

COLOR
Green

SCRIPTURE READINGS
Exodus 3:1-15; Psalm 105:1-6, 23-26, 45c; Romans 12:9-21; Matthew 16:21-28

THEME IDEAS
Woven through three of these scriptures is the theme of moving through and overcoming trials: as God sees the suffering of the Israelites and calls Moses to lead them from slavery to freedom; as Paul instructs the early church on how to endure suffering—staying humble, caring for others, choosing good over bitterness; as Jesus prepares his friends for his suffering, death, and resurrection, not even deterred by Peter's fear and discomfort. Within that first theme lies a second theme: not letting ourselves be caught up in bitterness or vengeance but leaving the judgment of foes for God to handle. Perhaps both themes may be accented by the words of the psalmist to sing of God's miracles, remember God's faithfulness, and seek God's strength to carry us through.

AUGUST 30, 2026

INVITATION AND GATHERING

CENTERING WORDS (Exodus 3:7-8)
Then the Lord said, "I have observed the misery of my people.... I have heard their cry on account of their taskmasters. Indeed, I know their sufferings, and I have come down to deliver them... and to bring them up out of that land to a good and broad land, a land flowing with milk and honey...."

CALL TO WORSHIP (Psalm 105)
O give thanks to the Lord.
We call on God's name.
Make known the deeds of our Creator,
singing them into the world.
Sing to God, O people.
We will sing praise—
to tell of God's wondrous works,
and give thanks for so many miracles.
Come, and seek the presence of the Lord—
and glory in God's holy name.
Let the hearts of all who seek the Holy rejoice,
for God brings strength to all the people.

OPENING PRAYER (Exodus 3)
Creator God, who shall we say that you are?
By what name can we call you—
    that would be enough to speak of all that you are
    and all that you shall be?
We can only call you 'I Am,'
    for you Were—and Are—
    and always Will Be—the Holy One.
You call us by name and invite us to come to you.
We answer, "Here I am," and come to stand
    on holy ground.
May we remember that all ground is holy ground,
for you are in all times and places—
    calling us to our lives each moment. Amen.

PROCLAMATION AND RESPONSE

PRAYER OF YEARNING (Psalm 105, Romans 12, Matthew 16)
God of our ancestors, God of us,
>we long to live as you call us to do,
>>letting love be true,
>>hating what is evil,
>>>and holding fast to what is good.

But we do not always manage to tell what is evil
>and what is good.

We do not always manage to choose
>that which gives life rather than steals it.

And so we become a stumbling block,
>when we mean to be a stepping stone.

God of our hearts, we yearn for your strength
>to let go the evil and choose the good.

We seek your presence
>to stay with us in our own suffering
>>and to keep us present to the suffering
>>>of others.

We long for you to take our struggles
>and turn them into strengths.

We ache to take our stumbling
>and turn it to steps on the journey,
>>growing nearer to you. Amen.

WORDS OF ASSURANCE (Exodus 3, Romans 12)
God of our lives,
>we have cried to you in our pain.

You have heard our suffering
>and stayed with us through our struggle.

You have never left us alone.

When we have been hungry,
>you have fed us.

When we have been thirsty,
>you have refreshed us.

When we have been angry,
> you have brought us to peace.

You give us patience, God,
> and help us to persevere
> > until you and we can rejoice again in hope.

PASSING THE PEACE OF CHRIST (Romans 12)
Family in faith, rejoice with those who rejoice, weep with those who weep . . . and so far, as it depends on you, live peaceably with all.

PRAYER OF PREPARATION (Psalm 19)
May the words of my mouth . . .
> **and the meditations of our hearts**
> **be acceptable in your sight, O Lord,**
> **our strength and our redeemer. Amen.**

RESPONSE TO THE WORD (Matthew 16, Romans 12)
We have heard God's word speaking to us.
Now let us live—
> as stepping stones,
> > rather than as stumbling blocks;
>
> in genuine love,
> > holding fast to all that is good;
>
> rejoicing in hope;
> seeking patience and peace in suffering;
> persevering in prayer.

In this day and all days. Amen.

THANKSGIVING AND COMMUNION

INVITATION TO THE OFFERING (Exodus 3)
God has given us blessings, both good and broad. Blessings overflowing like milk and honey. Let those blessings flow now—from our hearts and our lives—and into the world.

OFFERING PRAYER (Psalm 105)
Gracious God, you have done marvelous things,
   wonderous works for us
   and for all your people.
May we make your deeds known—
   your miracles told and your glory sung
   in our prayer and praise.
May your blessings flow through our lives
   and into the world. Amen.

SENDING FORTH

BENEDICTION (Romans 12)
People of God, live in harmony with one another
   and peaceably with all.
Go forth, to serve in genuine love. Amen.

AUGUST 30, 2026

Notes

September 6, 2026

Fifteenth Sunday after Pentecost
Proper 18

LeighAnn Shaw

COLOR
Green

SCRIPTURE READINGS
Exodus 12:1-14; Psalm 149; Romans 13:8-14; Matthew 18:15-20

THEME IDEAS
While diverse, these passages interweave a reminder of God's deliverance and redemption, God's justice and the urgency of love and the moral life. God's people are challenged to put on the spirit of light, love, and justice.

INVITATION AND GATHERING

CENTERING WORDS (Romans 13)
Awaken to the call of love, for love fulfills the law. Live fully in the light, as children of the day, embracing the grace and hope of our salvation.

SEPTEMBER 6, 2026

CALL TO WORSHIP (Romans 13)
    The night is nearly over; the day is almost here.
        We lay aside the deeds of darkness
        and put on the armor of light.
    We owe no one anything, except to love one another,
    for love is the fulfillment of the law.
        We come to worship with hearts awakened,
        ready to cast off the old and embrace the new.
    Let us awaken to the call of God,
    to live as people of the day,
    and to shine God's love in all we do.
        We worship the One who calls us into the light,
        to love one another as God has loved us. Amen.

OPENING PRAYER (Romans 13)
    Loving God, as we gather in your presence,
        we seek to put on the armor of light,
            and to live as your children.
    Help us cast aside the darkness
        and embrace the love that fulfills our law.
    Awaken us to your call,
        that we may walk in the light of Christ each day.
    In Jesus' name, we pray. Amen.

PROCLAMATION AND RESPONSE

PRAYER OF CONFESSION (Matthew 18)
    Merciful God, we have not always sought reconciliation
        as you have called us to do.
    We have allowed pride and fear
        to keep us from addressing conflicts
            with love and grace.
    Forgive the times we have withheld forgiveness
        and failed to seek peace.
    Helps us approach others with an open heart,
        ready to heal and restore relationships. Amen.

WORDS OF ASSURANCE (Matthew 18)
Hear the good news:
>Where two or three are gathered in God's name,
>God is there among us.
When we seek reconciliation, God is present,
>offering grace and healing.
In Christ, we are forgiven and restored,
>called to live in peace with one another.
Embrace this mercy and know that through God's love,
>all of us—beloved children of God—
>are made whole. Amen.

PASSING THE PEACE OF CHRIST (Matthew 18)
Jesus teaches us the importance of reconciliation and being in harmony with one another. When we seek peace and understanding, Christ is present among us, bringing healing and unity. As we pass the peace of Christ today, let us do so with open hearts, ready to forgive, ready to listen, and ready to love as Christ has loved us.

The peace of Christ be with you all.
And also with you.
Let us extend the peace of Christ with one another.

RESPONSE TO THE WORD (Romans 13, Matthew 18)
We are called to love one another,
and to seek reconciliation in all our relationships.
Let us walk in the light of Christ,
living in love, peace, and grace,
as we build a community of unity
and understanding.

AFFIRMATION OF FAITH (Matthew 18)
We believe in a God who calls us to be a people of reconciliation, reflecting the love and grace of Christ in all our relationships. Guided by the teachings of Jesus, we affirm the importance of seeking peace and understanding within our families, our communities, and our nation.

We believe that true faith is lived out in the pursuit of harmony, where conflicts are addressed with honesty, love, and a commitment to restoration. We affirm that God is present when we gather in the spirit of reconciliation, leading us toward unity and healing.

We commit ourselves to the work of mending broken relationships, building bridges where there are divides, and fostering a spirit of forgiveness and compassion. We believe that in doing so, we embody the light of Christ, bringing hope and peace to a world in need.

This is our faith: rooted in love, expressed in grace, and lived out in the pursuit of reconciliation for the glory of God. Amen.

THANKSGIVING AND COMMUNION

INVITATION TO THE OFFERING (Matthew 18)
Jesus calls us to be peacemakers, to seek reconciliation and healing in our relationships. As we offer our gifts today, let us also offer our hearts, committed to living out the love and grace that Christ has shown us. In giving our time, talents, and resources, we take part in God's work of restoration and peace in the world. Let our offerings reflect our desire to mend what is broken, to build up what has been torn down, and to bring hope where there is despair. As we give, may we also take action—seeking reconciliation with those from whom we are estranged, offering forgiveness, and striving to live in harmony with one another.
Let us give generously, as an expression of our commitment to Christ's ministry of peace and reconciliation. Amen.

OFFERING PRAYER (Matthew 18)
Gracious and reconciling God,
we bring these gifts before you
as a symbol of our commitment to your work
of peace and unity in the world.
Just as you ask us to seek reconciliation
with one another, we dedicate these offerings
to the ministry of healing and restoration
in our community and beyond.
Bless these gifts, Lord,
that they may build bridges where there are divides,
bring hope where there is hurt,
and extend your love to all.
As we offer our resources, may we also offer our hearts,
striving to live in harmony and peace,
as Christ has taught us. Amen.
Guide us in using these gifts wisely,
that your will may be done on earth
as it is in heaven. Amen.

SENDING FORTH

BENEDICTION (Matthew 18)
Go now with hearts open to reconciliation and peace.
As Christ is present whenever two or three are gathered
in the name of love, may you seek this presence
in all your relationships.
Walk in love, speak the truth with grace,
and strive to live in harmony with one another.
And may the peace of Christ,
which surpasses all understanding,
guard your hearts and minds
as you go forth to serve in love and unity. Amen.

SEPTEMBER 6, 2026

Notes

193

September 13, 2026

Sixteenth Sunday after Pentecost
Proper 19

Mary Scifres
Copyright © Mary Scifres

COLOR

Green

SCRIPTURE READINGS

Exodus 14:19-31; Exodus 15:1b-11, 20-21; Romans 14:1-12; Matthew 18:21-35

THEME IDEAS

The forgiveness theme of Matthew's gospel offers quite a contrast to the triumphalism of deliverance expressed in Exodus. Likewise, the call to acceptance and living only for God expressed in Romans 14 doesn't have much parallel to Exodus 14; yet the deliverance from slavery is the defining moment of the Hebrew people, Jesus' people and ancestors of the Christian people. Even when forgiving and accepting, we are reminded that oppression and injustice call for different values and different perspectives. Scripture is complex, speaking to many different situations and teaching even contradictory lessons. Scripture demands that our theology be equally complex and diverse.

SEPTEMBER 13, 2026

INVITATION AND GATHERING

CENTERING WORDS *(Exodus 14, Romans 14, Matthew 18)*
Forgiveness is a complex notion. Forgiving ourselves and forgiving others can be equally challenging, but even more so when oppression and injustice are part of the story. May God guide our forgiving and our living, to embrace the deeper truth of Christ's teachings.

CALL TO WORSHIP *(Exodus 15)*
Sing praise to God,
our Creator and Redeemer.
Sing praise to Christ,
our Lord and Savior.
Sing praise to the Spirit,
who has called us to worship this day.

OPENING PRAYER *(Romans 14, Matthew 18)*
Loving God, thank you for the great mercy and grace
that draw us close to your holiness.
Flow through our worship and through our lives
with your holy presence and your forgiving grace,
that we may be people of holy love
and gracious forgiveness.
In your holy name, we pray. Amen.

PROCLAMATION AND RESPONSE

PRAYER OF YEARNING *(Romans 14, Matthew 18)*
Gracious God, we want to be as grace-filled
with ourselves and with others as you are.
But honestly, it's easier to sing about grace
than it is to offer it freely and abundantly.

Help us put our songs into action,
> our words of yearning into lives filled with mercy
>> and forgiveness—for ourselves and for others.
One time, seven times, or seventy-seven times,
> each moment of grace matters and makes us better.
Let your grace flow through our lives so abundantly
> that it overflows into every situation,
>> protecting and preserving everyone it touches.
In your love and grace, we pray. Amen.

WORDS OF ASSURANCE (Romans 14)
My friends, we belong to God, we belong to Christ.
Christ's amazing grace saves and redeems.
Christ's grace is enough for all.

PASSING THE PEACE OF CHRIST (Romans 14, Matthew 18)
Forgiven and loved, we are invited to share signs of forgiveness and love with one another as we pass the peace of Christ.

RESPONSE TO THE WORD (Matthew 18, Luke 11:4)
Gracious God, forgive our sins
> as we forgive those who sin against us.
These familiar words can trip us up in daily life,
> yet they are the words Christ Jesus taught us to pray.
Help us live the words we pray,
> and accept the gift that forgiveness can be
>> in our lives and in our world. Amen.

THANKSGIVING AND COMMUNION

INVITATION TO THE OFFERING (Romans 14)
In our lives, we live for the Lord. In our offerings, we give for God. May our lives and our generosity reflect our commitment to these truths.

OFFERING PRAYER *(Romans 14, Matthew 18)*
    Thank you for the generosity of your love,
        forgiveness, and grace, dear God.
    Thank you for trusting us to share this generosity
        with others.
    Bless our offerings with grace, forgiveness, and love.
    Bless our lives, our giving, and our actions,
        that they may reflect and share these gifts
        in all that we say and in all that we do. Amen.

SENDING FORTH

BENEDICTION *(Romans 14, Matthew 18)*
    Forgiven and loved,
        we go into the world with forgiveness and love.
    Blessed beyond measure,
        we will share our blessings with generosity
        and joy.

(For resources related to today's Exodus readings, consult The Abingdon Worship Annual 2023 *or* 2020, *or visit www.creativeworshipmadeeasy.com)*

Notes

September 20, 2026

Seventeenth Sunday after Pentecost
Proper 20

Karen Clark Ristine

COLOR
Green

SCRIPTURE READINGS
Exodus 16:2-15; Psalm 105:1-6, 37-45; Philippians 1:21-30; Matthew 20:1-16

THEME IDEAS
Like the followers of Moses in the wilderness, like the laborers in the field in the parable of Jesus, we sometimes grumble and complain when life seems harder than we want or expect. Each scripture this week has a common theme of presence. Divine Presence, yes, and also our presence with one another. Paul describes following in Christ's way as struggle—a struggle we share together. Jesus invites us to understand that grace is given to all, far beyond our human understanding of equity.

INVITATION AND GATHERING

CENTERING WORDS *(Philippians 1:27, NRSV)*
"Live your life in a manner worthy of the gospel of Christ."

CALL TO WORSHIP *(Exodus 16, Philippians 1, Matthew 20)*
In their wilderness wandering, the Israelites grumbled.
The Lord lighted their way and provided nourishment.
**In our life journeys, we will give thanks
for the providence of the Holy One.**
In their daily work, the laborers in the field grumbled
with resentment over gracious giving.
**In our daily lives, we will rejoice at generosity
shown to others.**
As we seek to live our lives by the example of Christ,
may we delight in God's grace.
**We will offer caring presence
and abundant generosity.
We will even endeavor to give up our grumbling.**

OPENING PRAYER *(Exodus 16, Philippians 1)*
Gracious and Loving God, we give thanks
for the many ways we see your abiding presence
throughout scripture and within our own lives.
You hear not only our praise
but also our complaints.
Teach us to hear our own grumbling
as a signifier to redirect our thoughts and lives
to gratitude and generosity.
In hearing our own complaints,
may we look to Christ Jesus for examples of grace
And may we follow your Holy Spirit
to offer presence to one another,
as we walk in faith together. Amen.

SEPTEMBER 20, 2026

PROCLAMATION AND RESPONSE

PRAYER OF YEARNING (Matthew 20)
   Our greatest hope, O God, is to love as Jesus did,
      with grace and compassion.
   Clear the wandering paths of our minds and hearts,
      that your Spirit may fill us with grace
         to receive and share your blessings. Amen.

WORDS OF ASSURANCE (Exodus 16, Matthew 20)
   The Lord heard the complaints of the Israelites and offered guiding presence. Jesus calls us to celebrate generosity and grace, not just in our own lives but in the lives of others. Know this: In all things, the Lord hears us, sees us, and loves us just as we are.

   In the name of Jesus Christ, you are forgiven.
   In the name of Jesus Christ, you are forgiven.

RESPONSE TO THE WORD (Exodus 16, Philippians 1, Matthew 20)
   In gratitude for the presence of the Divine
      and for the teachings of Jesus,
         may Spirit guide us to live lives
            worthy of the gospel of Christ.

THANKSGIVING AND COMMUNION

OFFERING PRAYER (Exodus 16)
   We offer these gifts, O God,
      in gratitude for your provision in our lives.
   We offer tangible gifts of money, where we are able,
      and tangible gifts of our time, our prayers,
         our service, and our witness
            to your abundant grace. Amen.

SENDING FORTH

BENEDICTION
Go now in the name of the God who goes before us,
and in the name of Christ, whose love and grace
abound within us.
Go seeking the call of Spirit to a place
beyond complaint, a place of gratitude.
Go in peace. Amen.

Notes

September 27, 2026

Eighteenth Sunday after Pentecost
Proper 21

Karen Clark Ristine

COLOR
Green

SCRIPTURE READINGS
Exodus 17:1-7; Psalm 78:1-4, 12-16; Philippians 2:1-13; Matthew 21:23-32

THEME IDEAS
Listening and discerning and setting self aside fill the lectionary passages this week. Moses listened to God in the face of angry followers. The psalmist invites us to listen for the presence of the Divine One. Philippians encourages us to set ourselves aside, working out our own salvation with awareness of God at work within us. And this complex passage from Matthew includes the admonition from Jesus to listen to prophets sent by God, and to serve with integrity. Listen, discern, act selflessly.

INVITATION AND GATHERING

CENTERING WORDS (*Philippians 2:5, NRSV*)
"Let the same mind be in you that was in Christ Jesus."

CALL TO WORSHIP *(Exodus 17, Psalm 78, Philippians 2)*
Moses listened to the guidance of the Lord
rather than the quarreling of the people.
We will set aside our grumbling and quarrels,
that we may hear the voice of God more clearly.
The poetry of the psalmist invites us to "give ear"
to Divine teaching.
We will incline our ears, and listen for ways
to share the presence of God.
The letter to the Philippians encourages them and us
to have the same mind as Christ,
and to empty ourselves, that we might be filled.
We will humble ourselves as Christ was humble,
opening our very lives to the ongoing call of God.

OPENING PRAYER *(Exodus 17, Psalm 78)*
Guiding God, you led our ancestors in faith
through the wilderness as a pillar of cloud by day
and a fiery pillar by night.
You quenched their thirst and shared manna
to satisfy their hunger.
We often wish we could see you now
in such celestial wonders.
Yet we know you are near.
We feel your Spirit presence, sustaining us
along life's journey. Amen.

PROCLAMATION AND RESPONSE

PRAYER OF CONFESSION or PRAYER OF YEARNING
(Exodus 17, Philippians 2)
We long to quiet the noise and distraction of daily life,
to hear more clearly your call on our lives.
Still our souls, that we may hear with clarity
the wonders of your love guiding us on. Amen.

WORDS OF ASSURANCE (Philippians 2)
    Jesus, in human form, humbled himself before God.
    God, who is at work in you,
        invites you to humble self-awareness.
    Spirit nudges your will in ways that lead to goodness.
    None of us are alone in this walk of faith.
    So, hear and believe: In the name of Jesus Christ
    you are forgiven
    In the name of Jesus Christ, you are forgiven.

RESPONSE TO THE WORD (Exodus 17, Psalm 78)
    Speak, for your servants are listening.
    We long to hear and know and act,
        guided by scripture and by our awareness
        of your presence in our lives and times.

THANKSGIVING AND COMMUNION

OFFERING PRAYER (Philippians 2)
    We offer these our gifts, Holy One,
        and we also offer our lives in mind, body, and spirit.
    We endeavor to have the same mind as Christ,
        that our actions, through faith, might serve you
            with humility.

SENDING FORTH

BENEDICTION (Exodus 17, Philippians 2)
    Go into your lives, listening for the call of God.
    Go into your communities with Christ-like humbleness.
    Give ear to the whispers and shouts of the Holy Spirit.
    Go in peace and stay in courage. Amen.

Notes

October 4, 2026

Nineteenth Sunday after Pentecost
World Communion Sunday / Proper 22

Karin Ellis

COLOR
Green

SCRIPTURE READINGS
Exodus 20:1-4, 7-9, 12-20; Psalm 19; Philippians 3:4b-14; Matthew 21:33-46

THEME IDEAS
On this World Communion Sunday, the scriptures remind us that living in the ways of God help to build up the community, and eventually the world. The passage from Exodus recounts the receiving of the Ten Commandments from God. These laws are set before the community to order their lives with one another and with God. The psalmist sings of how the earth proclaims the glory of God, while the people are expected to keep the commands of the Lord. Paul writes to remind the Philippians why he follows Christ and why he keeps striving to live in the ways of Christ. And Jesus tells a story about a landowner which reminds the hearers how important it is to take care of and nurture what God has given to us, namely his Son, Jesus Christ.

INVITATION AND GATHERING

CENTERING WORDS *(Psalm 19, Philippians 3)*
We gather to learn about God. We gather to know Christ more deeply. We gather to remember and give thanks that we are a part of the community of faith—a community that reaches around the world.

CALL TO WORSHIP *(Psalm 19)*
The heavens proclaim the glory of God!
We too proclaim what God has done in our lives.
Voices of praise shout to the ends of the earth.
**May we join the chorus,
as we sing of God's great and abiding love!**

OPENING PRAYER *(Psalm 19, Matthew 21)*
Creating God, like the earth around us,
    we gather to proclaim your glory.
We pray that you will revive our souls today.
We pray that you will help us become a little bit wiser.
We pray that our hearts will rejoice
    at the sound of your name.
We pray that our eyes will be opened to your ways.
We pray that we might live in peace and harmony
    with one another.
And we pray that today, and every day,
    we will again choose to follow in the ways of Christ,
        so that our lives may become an example
            of your love and grace to the world.
In the name of Christ, we pray. Amen.

PROCLAMATION AND RESPONSE

PRAYER OF CONFESSION *(Exodus 20)*
God of grace, from the very beginning,
    you have watched over your people

      and given them ways to live in harmony
         with one another.
  But too often we have forgotten your ways.
  Forgive us for mocking your holy name.
  Forgive us for harming others and ourselves.
  Forgive us for stealing ideas and property from others.
  Forgive us for being jealous.
  Forgive us for neglecting to rest our bodies, minds
      and spirits.
  Forgive us for turning away from you.
  Holy One, grant us your mercy,
      and help us live again in your ways
         of love and grace. Amen.

WORDS OF ASSURANCE *(Psalm 19, Philippians 3)*
  Brother and sisters and siblings in Christ,
      God will wipe away all our faults.
  Know that the grace and mercy of God
      are never far from us, and that God desires
         that we live in righteousness.
  In the name of the risen Christ, you are forgiven.
  Thanks be to God. Amen.

PASSING THE PEACE OF CHRIST *(Psalm 19)*
  Friends, there is no place on earth where God's glory is not proclaimed. Knowing this, let us joyfully turn to one another and proclaim the peace of Christ.

  May the peace of Christ be with you.
  And also with you!

PRAYER OF PREPARATION *(Psalm 19, Matthew 21)*
  O Lord, we are told that your words are sweeter than honey. May the words that are spoken, and the prayers in our hearts, be pleasing to you, our cornerstone. Amen.

RESPONSE TO THE WORD *(Philippians 3, Matthew 21)*
May these words inspire us to strive for the prize
of living in the ways of Christ.
**And may we be empowered to bear good fruit f
or the kingdom of God.**

THANKSGIVING

INVITATION TO THE OFFERING *(Philippians 3)*
In our effort to know Christ, we realize how much God has given to us. May we offer a portion of our gifts to God in thanksgiving and praise for all we have been given.

OFFERING PRAYER *(Matthew 21)*
Holy One, creator of all, we give you thanks
for all you have entrusted to us.
As good stewards, we now bring you these gifts
and ask that you use them to help your children
around the world.
As we bring our gifts, we also offer our lives,
praying that you will use us to bear good fruit
for all people. Amen.

SENDING FORTH

BENEDICTION
May the glory of our Creator be ever present with you.
May the peace of Christ become the foundation
of your life.
And may the Holy Spirit empower you to keep striving
for the ways of Christ.
Go in peace. Amen.

OCTOBER 4, 2026

Notes

October 11, 2026

Twentieth Sunday after Pentecost
Proper 23

Michael Beu
Copyright © Michael Beu

COLOR

Green

SCRIPTURE READINGS

Exodus 32:1-14; Psalm 106:1-6, 19-23; Philippians 4:1-9; Matthew 22:1-14

THEME IDEAS

We are to praise God and rejoice in the Lord always. The Hebrews who traveled in the time of the Exodus knew this, but when Moses took so long coming down the mountain of God, they decided new gods were in order. This was clearly not their best decision. The psalmist exhorts the people to praise the Lord, because God is good. God's faithful love endures forever. Philippians exhorts the people to rejoice in God and be glad, focusing our thoughts and attentions on the things that are good and honorable and just. Matthew's Gospel recounts a baffling tale of a king burning down the city of those who refuse to come to a royal wedding. The king then invites those on the highways and byways, only to toss out a conscripted guest for lacking proper wedding clothes.

OCTOBER 11, 2026

INVITATION AND GATHERING

CENTERING WORDS *(Psalm 106, Philippians 4)*
Rejoice in the Lord always. Rejoice in the Lord. Rejoice.

CALL TO WORSHIP *(Philippians 4)*
Rejoice in God always!
Rejoice in God's steadfast love.
Rejoice in Christ's enduring grace.
Rejoice in God's saving Word.
Rejoice in the Spirit's gentle guidance.
Rejoice in God's healing presence.
Again, I say, rejoice!

OPENING PRAYER *(Psalm 106, Philippians 4)*
Holy God, we come into your house
   with praise on our lips
      and songs of joy in our hearts.
We come to stand firm in our conviction:
   that good is stronger than evil,
   that love is stronger than hate,
   that truth will ultimately win the day.
We come to be grounded in Christ.

PROCLAMATION AND RESPONSE

PRAYER OF YEARNING *(Exodus 32, Philippians 4)*
Holy Presence, following you is seldom easy.
When worry and doubt cloud our vision
   bless us with your peace.
When work and social obligations rob our strength,
   grant us rest.
We yearn to focus our hearts and minds
   on things that are excellent, admirable,
      and worthy of praise.
Shine the light of your love in our lives,
   that we may bring your light to the world. Amen.

WORDS OF ASSURANCE (Philippians 4)
    The peace of God, which surpasses all understanding,
        is ours through Christ Jesus.
    In Christ, we rest secure.

PASSING THE PEACE OF CHRIST (Philippians 4)
    When we keep our hearts and minds focused on things that are excellent and admirable, God blesses us with a peace that passes all understanding. Let us share signs of this peace with one another.

INVITATION TO THE WORD (Philippians 4)
    As we listen for the word of God, let us focus our hearts and minds on things that are honorable and true, just and pure, pleasing and commendable, excellent and worthy of praise.

RESPONSE TO THE WORD (Philippians 4)
    Bathe us in your compassion and love, Holy One.
    Clothe us in your justice and righteousness.
    Dress us in your mercy and grace,
    that our hearts and find peace in in you. Amen.

THANKSGIVING AND COMMUNION

INVITATION TO THE OFFERING (Psalm 106)
    God's steadfast love endures forever. As recipients of God's love and grace, let us show our gratitude for the God's many blessings by giving of our tithes and offering.

OFFERING PRAYER (Psalm 106, Philippians 4)
    God of steadfast love, your blessings overwhelm us.
    For the abundant gifts in our lives,
        we thank you.
    For the peace that passes all understanding,
        we praise you.
    For keeping our hearts and minds in Christ Jesus,
        we honor you.

Receive the gifts we bring you this day,
    and help us stay focused
        on things that are excellent and admirable,
            holy and just, righteous and pure. Amen.

SENDING FORTH

BENEDICTION (Philippians 4)
    May the peace of God,
        which surpasses all understanding,
        keep your hearts and minds in Christ Jesus,
        from this day forward and forevermore. Amen.

Notes

October 18, 2026

Twenty-First Sunday after Pentecost
Proper 24

Michael Beu
Copyright © Michael Beu

COLOR

Green

SCRIPTURE READINGS

Exodus 33:12-23; Psalm 99; 1 Thessalonians 1:1-10; Matthew 22:15-22

THEME IDEAS

The glory and power of God unites these readings. Moses yearns to know God more intimately and to behold God's glorious presence. The psalmist speaks of God enthroned with the cherubim and seraphim while the nations quake. Paul proclaims that the good news did not just come to the church with words but with the power of the Holy Spirit. Finally, when Jesus was tested by the Pharisees, he made it clear that just as Caesar is due the coin he mints to his glory, God is due the honor and glory that belongs to God. We may not be able to see God face-to-face, but we can all seek God's glorious presence with thanksgiving and praise.

OCTOBER 18, 2026

INVITATION AND GATHERING

CENTERING WORDS *(Exodus 33, Psalm 99, 1 Thessalonians 1)*
Hear God's call to be more than we have become. Be inspired anew to live in God's service.

CALL TO WORSHIP *(Exodus 33, Psalm 99, Matthew 22)*
May the nations quake and the peoples tremble.
God sits enthroned in the heavens,
bringing justice and righteousness.
May the mountains tremble and the seas roar.
God's glory is stronger than the foundation
of the earth.
May the humble seek the living God.
God's goodness and mercy sustain the faithful
in times of trial.
Come, let us worship the Lord.

OPENING PRAYER *(Exodus 33, 1 Thessalonians 1)*
Mighty God, awe us with your glory
as you pass before us,
and reveal the radiance of your presence.
May we embody your word
as we strive to live as a holy people,
and as we seek to share your message of love
with the world. Amen.

PROCLAMATION AND RESPONSE

PRAYER OF YEARNING *(Exodus 33, Matthew 22)*
Gracious and merciful God,
temper our certitude with humility and grace.
When we fail to discover our own errors,
open our hearts to your wisdom.

For we yearn to follow your ways more nearly
and perceive your presence more clearly.
Come to us with gentle correction,
that we may truly bring your good news
to a world in need. Amen.

WORDS OF ASSURANCE (*Exodus 33, Psalm 99*)
When we call, God answers.
When we seek, we are sure to find.
Call to God and seek the Lord with your whole heart.

PASSING THE PEACE OF CHRIST (*Matthew 22*)
When we give to God the things that belong to God, the most wonderful sense of peace washes over us. Let us share this moment of grace as we pass the peace of Christ.

RESPONSE TO THE WORD (*1 Thessalonians 1, Matthew 22*)
God of grace and God of glory,
bless our lives with your presence,
and lead our actions
through your abiding word.
Bless our faith with your Spirit,
that we may be constant
in our prayers and devotions,
through Jesus Christ, our Lord. Amen.

THANKSGIVING AND COMMUNION

OFFERING PRAYER (*1 Thessalonians 1, Matthew 22*)
God of manifold blessings,
enrich the works of our hands,
that we may speak your truth
and share your love with the world.
Accept and bless these gifts,
that they may aid those in need,
even as they are visible signs
of the honor you are due. Amen.

OCTOBER 18, 2026

SENDING FORTH

BENEDICTION (1 Thessalonians 1)
Strengthened by the presence of God,
we go forth in hope.
Guided by the teachings of Christ,
we go forth to serve.
Led by the power of the Holy Spirit,
we go forth to love.

Notes

October 25, 2026

Twenty-Second Sunday after Pentecost
Reformation Sunday / Proper 25

Mary Scifres
Copyright © Mary Scifres

COLOR
Green

SCRIPTURE READINGS
Deuteronomy 34:1-12; Psalm 90:1-6, 13-17;
1 Thessalonians 2:1-8; Matthew 22:34-46

THEME IDEAS
Even in this ordinary season, common threads can be found in today's scriptures. In particular, the leaders in these scriptures are connected to the ancient story of God's people—first led by Moses, then Joshua, centuries later by the Pharisees, and now a new flock being led by Jesus, and eventually Paul. The diverse leadership brought by these men finds a common theme of Torah first brought off the mountain by Moses and now summarized by Jesus: Love God, love your neighbor. "All the Law and the Prophets depend on these two commands" (Matthew 22:38-40).

OCTOBER 25, 2026

INVITATION AND GATHERING

CENTERING WORDS *(Matthew 22)*
Love God with all your heart, mind, soul, and strength. Love your neighbor as you love yourself. Sounds so simple, but turns out to be kind of complex.

CALL TO WORSHIP *(Deuteronomy 34, Psalm 90, Matthew 22)*
Come to us, O God.
**Breathe through our worship
with your Holy Spirit.**
Fill us with your faithful love.
Guide us with your ancient teachings.
Come to us, O God.
Be in our prayer and praise.

OPENING PRAYER *(Deuteronomy 34, Psalm 90, Matthew 22)*
God of ages past and days to come,
　help us embrace both your ancient wisdom
　　and your ongoing guidance.
Help us hear anew your words from years gone by.
Open our hearts and minds
　to fully embrace what it means to love you,
　　to love ourselves, and to love our neighbors
　　　as you have loved us.
In love and gratitude, we pray. Amen.

PROCLAMATION AND RESPONSE

PRAYER OF YEARNING *(Psalm 90)*
O God, our help and hope, you have been with us
　from the first moment of creation,
　　forming and teaching us to be your people,
　　　to walk in your ways,
　　　　and to live in your love.

Come back quickly to us when we turn away.
Give us your compassion and mercy
> when we feel lost and forsaken.
Fill us with your faithful love
> and your generous kindness,
>> that our lives may be full and fulfilling,
>>> and that the work of our hands
>>>> may be your work in the world.
In your loving name, we pray. Amen.

WORDS OF ASSURANCE (Psalm 90)
God has been our help and our hope
> from generation to generation.
God continues to be our help and our hope,
> both now and forevermore.

RESPONSE TO THE WORD (Deuteronomy 34, Psalm 90, Matthew 22)
Before the mountains were born,
> **God was present and dreaming of us.**

Before the law was given,
> **God's love was present and blessing us.**

Before we knew God's love,
> **God's love knew us.**

And now God invites us to live in this love
> **and to share it abundantly with all.**

May we be children of love
> **who bring love to God's world.**

THANKSGIVING AND COMMUNION

OFFERING PRAYER (Matthew 22)
Gracious God, bless the offerings of ourselves
> and our gifts.
May they be offerings of love,
> for you and for your people.
In loving gratitude, we pray. Amen.

OCTOBER 25, 2026

SENDING FORTH

BENEDICTION *(1 Thessalonians 2, Matthew 22)*
As beloved children of God,
   let's go to bring God's love to the world.
Led by the teachings of Christ,
   let's go to live the lessons of love, justice, and grace.

Notes

November 1, 2026

Twenty-Third Sunday after Pentecost
Proper 26 / All Saints Sunday

Mary Scifres
Copyright © Mary Scifres

COLOR
White

SCRIPTURE READINGS
Revelation 7:9-17; Psalm 34:1-10, 22; 1 John 3:1-3; Matthew 5:1-12

THEME IDEAS
The gift of God's blessings, both in this life and in the next, is borne out of great hardship. Each of today's readings point to the paradox that sainthood doesn't come easily, nor do the blessings of life. Even the lives of love we lead as God's children are all too often misunderstood or even rejected. Yet, blessed we are—as are the saints who have gone before us—for we have known God's love, and that is blessing enough.

INVITATION AND GATHERING

CENTERING WORDS (Psalm 34, 1 John 3)
Blessed be the Lord, and all of God's beloved people. Blessed by love, we are blessed indeed.

CALL TO WORSHIP *(Revelation 7, Psalm 34, 1 John 3)*
    Bless the Lord, whose love shines upon us.
    Bless the Lord, my soul!
    Bless our lives, that reflect God's love.
    Bless the Lord, my soul!
    Bless our worship, that it may glorify God.
    Bless the Lord, my soul!

OPENING PRAYER *(Revelation 7, 1 John 3, Matthew 5)*
    Glorious God, we come into your holy presence
        with joy and gratitude.
    Bless this time of worship to draw us closer to you.
    Bless our lives to shine brightly with your love.
    Bless our work in the world to bring your justice
        and compassion to life.
    In your holy name, we pray. Amen.

PROCLAMATION AND RESPONSE

PRAYER OF YEARNING *(1 John 3, Matthew 5, All Saints Day)*
    Sainthood is hard!
    Yet, you call us to live into your blessings
        by loving and caring for all of your creation.
    Give us strength to answer our call.
    Give us wisdom to live your teachings.
    Give us courage to withstand the trials
        and tribulations of life.
    Give us humility to embrace sainthood,
        even when our sins and shortcomings haunt our days
        and cause us to judge ourselves and others.
    Love us into sainthood,
        that others may find us to be
            generous and compassionate friends.

WORDS OF ASSURANCE (1 John 3, Matthew 5, All Saints Day)
>God saves us again and again and again,
>>calling us to blessings and saintly living.
>
>This hope and this grace are enough to purify us,
>>even as Christ is pure.

RESPONSE TO THE WORD (1 John 3)
>See what kind of love God has given to us:
>>**Love that defines us as God's own children.**
>
>See what love invites us to live:
>>**Love that invites us to love all of God's people.**
>
>See what love redeems us and makes us whole:
>>**Love that invites us into the cloud of saints.**
>
>Thank God for this marvelous gift!

THANKSGIVING AND COMMUNION

OFFERING PRAYER (1 John 3, Matthew 5)
>Holy One, thank you for blessing us in so many ways.
>Please bless our offerings:
>>to bring your presence more fully into the world,
>>to spread your love to far and wide,
>>to bring hope and peace where despair runs deep.
>
>In loving gratitude, we pray. Amen.

INVITATION TO COMMUNION (Matthew 5, All Saints Day)
>You who are grieving and feeling hopeless,
>>**this table is set for you.**
>
>You who are humble and kind,
>>**this table is set for you.**
>
>You who are starving for justice,
>>**this table is set for you.**
>
>You who are yearning for peace,
>>**this table is set for you.**

You who are burdened and downtrodden,
this table is set for you.
You who are sinners and saints,
this table is set for you.

SENDING FORTH

BENEDICTION (1 John 3)
Dear friends, you are God's children.
The world needs God's children.
Go to make the world better with love,
for the world needs more love,
and we're the ones to bring it!

Notes

November 8, 2026

Twenty-Fourth Sunday after Pentecost
Proper 27

Michael Beu
Copyright © Michael Beu

COLOR

Green

SCRIPTURE READINGS

Joshua 24:1-3a, 14-25; Psalm 78:1-7;
1 Thessalonians 4:13-18; Matthew 25:1-13

THEME IDEAS

Choices have consequences. Choosing to follow God changes everything. Choosing to share the wisdom of God's holy mystery with the next generation provides our children a chance at a real future. Choosing to remain vigilant keeps us ready for when the bridegroom appears. Today's scriptures remind us that we need persistence, patience, and faithfulness for the long haul. But first and foremost, they remind us that it all begins with a choice: Whom will we serve?

NOVEMBER 8, 2026

INVITATION AND GATHERING

CENTERING WORDS *(Joshua 24, Psalm 78)*
God asks that we Choose this day whom we will follow and whom we will serve. Will we choose God? The choice is ours.

CALL TO WORSHIP *(Joshua 24, Psalm 78, 1 Thessalonians 4)*
The God of our ancestors has called us here.
We are witnesses.
The wisdom of the ages has called us here.
We are witnesses.
The choice to follow God has called us here.
We are witnesses.
The Lord of life has called us here.
We are witnesses.

OPENING PRAYER *(Joshua 24, Psalm 78, Matthew 25)*
Promise of the ages, we come to you this day
    to choose the ways of life.
Grant us patience in our waiting,
    as we watch for signs   of your coming kingdom.
We will teach our children your ways,
    and pass on the lessons of life and death
        we have learned. Amen.

PROCLAMATION AND RESPONSE

PRAYER OF YEARNING *(Joshua 24, Matthew 25)*
When our courage wears thin, O God,
    strengthen our resolve to choose you each day.
Steel us for the long watches of the night—
    for we long to be found ready
        when you appear in your glory.

Fill our lamps with your grace,
> that we might share your light with our children
> and with the generations that follow. Amen.

WORDS OF ASSURANCE (1 Thessalonians 4)
We worship a God of mercy and love.
Choose the Lord each day you will live.

PASSING THE PEACE OF CHRIST (Joshua 24, Matthew 25)
True peace is found when we choose life and follow God. True wisdom is found when we choose to wait for Christ, even when the hour is late. Turn to one another and share the deep peace and healing wisdom found in choosing God this day.

RESPONSE TO THE WORD (Joshua 24, Psalm 78, 1 Thessalonians 4, Matthew 25)
Have you made your choice?
We will walk with God.
Will you choose hope over despair?
We are prepared for the journey.
Are you ready to share the lessons you have learned?
We will teach our children the wisdom of old.

THANKSGIVING AND COMMUNION

INVITATION TO THE OFFERING (Matthew 25)
Whether wise or foolish, everyone needs oil for their lamps, food for their tables, and love for their lives. Let us share the bounty we have received, that no one may be left alone in the dark.

OFFERING PRAYER (Joshua 24)
We dedicate these gifts to you, Eternal One,
> as symbols of our choice to follow you.

Receive these gifts of love
> as celebrations of your presence in our lives.

Hold us to our promises,
  that we might share your blessings
  and wisdom with the world. Amen.

SENDING FORTH

BENEDICTION (Joshua 24, Matthew 25)
Choose God this day, and keep your lamps lit.
We go with hearts ablaze with God's love.
Choose God this day, and shine with God's light.
We go with lives kindled with the call to serve.
Choose God this day and enter into fullness of life.
We go to embrace the life we have received.

Notes

November 15, 2026

Twenty-Fifth Sunday after Pentecost
Proper 28

Mary Scifres
Copyright © Mary Scifres

COLOR

Green

SCRIPTURE READINGS

Judges 4:1-7; Psalm 123; 1 Thessalonians 5:1-11; Matthew 25:14-30

THEME IDEAS

The mystery of discerning God's guidance and wisdom flows through today's readings. A woman named Deborah is called to be both prophet and judge of Israel, bringing her wisdom and leadership as a mysterious blessing in the ancient patriarchal world. The Thessalonians are warned to be alert to the troubles that lure people into drunken-like stupor, recognizing that these will be signs for God's people to stay wide awake and alert for the day of the Lord. Jesus' parable of the talents rings down through the ages, with its mysterious lessons that both trouble and challenge us to make life-giving use of the blessings we are given. These scriptures bring mystery and confusion, even as they bring wisdom and guidance.

NOVEMBER 15, 2026

INVITATION AND GATHERING

CENTERING WORDS (1 Thessalonians 5)
Live with Christ. Look for Christ. Listen for Christ, and expect Christ's arrival to come in unexpected ways.

CALL TO WORSHIP (Psalm 123, Matthew 25)
Raise your eyes to the God of heaven and earth.
We raise our hearts and voices
with songs of praise.
Awaken your mind to the mysteries of God.
We open ourselves to listen and learn
in new ways.
Notice your blessings and gifts,
miraculously given by God.
We offer our lives and gifts to bless
and grow God's love in the world.

OPENING PRAYER (Judges 4, Matthew 25)
God of mystery and miracles,
   bless our worship with your presence.
Bless our lives with your guidance.
Bless our world with your wisdom.
May we perceive your mysterious ways
   as miracles and paths to draw us closer to you
      and to your realm here on earth.
In your holy name, we pray. Amen.

PROCLAMATION AND RESPONSE

PRAYER OF YEARNING (Judges 4, Matthew 25)
Wise One, we want to be wise like Deborah
   and the wise leaders of old.
We want to be wise like Jesus
   and the disciples who built your church.

We want to be wise like you,
>   but your ways are so mysterious,
>   they confuse sometimes.
> Guide us out of confusion.
> Help us see clearly and brightly,
>   led by the light of your Son, Christ Jesus.
> Strengthen us to live the wisdom you offer,
>   that our gifts and talents may grow and expand
>   your kingdom of love each day.
> In faith and trust, we pray. Amen.

WORDS OF ASSURANCE (1 Thessalonians 5)
> Jesus has raised us for new life.
> Jesus shines for us as a light in the dark
>   to help us find our way to God.

PASSING THE PEACE OF CHRIST (1 Thessalonians 5)
> Continue encouraging one another and building one another up as we share signs of peace and love together this day.

INTRODUCTION TO THE WORD (1 Thessalonians 5)
> Wake up! This is not nap time. This is deep listening time.
> Wake up, and listen for the word of God.

RESPONSE TO THE WORD (Matthew 25)
> One talent or ten, one gift or many,
> one blessing or abundant blessings,
>   **our lives and gifts are blessings to share.**
> One dollar or a million, one minute or 365 days,
> one cup of water or an entire feast,
>   **our lives and gifts are blessings to share.**
> May we recognize our blessings
> and be courageous in our sharing.
>   **May we embrace and share our gifts**
>   **to grow God's realm of love on this earth.**

NOVEMBER 15, 2026

THANKSGIVING AND COMMUNION

INVITATION TO THE OFFERING (Matthew 25)
One talent or ten, one dollar or a million, every gift matters to God and to our church. In this time of offering, let's reflect on the myriad ways in which God invites us to share ourselves and our gifts.

OFFERING PRAYER (1 Thessalonians 5, Matthew 25)
God of mystery and miracles,
    bless the gifts and lives we offer to you today
        with your miraculous abundance
        and your mysterious guidance.
Transform these gifts and lives
    to be instruments of your love, justice and mercy,
        that they might bring your realm to earth. Amen.

SENDING FORTH

BENEDICTION (1 Thessalonians 5, Matthew 25)
You know what time it is.
    It's time to get to work.
It's time to follow Christ.
    It's time to go where God leads.
It's time to offer ourselves.
    And time to bring love to the world.

Notes

November 22, 2026

Reign of Christ
Proper 29

B. J. Beu
Copyright © B. J. Beu

COLOR
White

SCRIPTURE READINGS
Ezekiel 34:11-16, 20-24; Psalm 100; Ephesians 1:15-23; Matthew 25:31-46

THEME IDEAS

O to be sheep in God's fold. In Ezekiel, God promises to gather the scattered and the lost sheep, bind the wounds of the injured, and bring justice to the fat sheep that have chased the weaker sheep away. It will be God who does this, not some hireling. The psalmist rejoices that we belong to God, our shepherd. In Ephesians, we are called to give thanks continually, for grace, light, and power has been given to us through Christ, who is above every ruler on earth. Finally, Matthew's Gospel continues the judgment motif seen in Ezekiel, and reminds us that our actions have eternal consequences. Our shepherd is righteous and just, and if we wish to abide in God's favor, we are charged to feed the hungry, clothe the naked, visit the sick and imprisoned, and comfort those who mourn.

INVITATION AND GATHERING

CENTERING WORDS *(Ezekiel 34, Psalm 100)*
Do you feel lost? Fear not, the Good Shepherd will lead you safely home.

CALL TO WORSHIP *(Psalm 100, Matthew 25)*
Enter God's gates with gladness,
and God's courts with praise.
Rejoice as God's people,
and rest as sheep in God's pasture.
Serve God with joyful hearts,
and worship God with justice and mercy.

OPENING PRAYER *(Ezekiel 34, Ephesians 1, Matthew 25)*
Glorious God, enlighten our eyes
to our hope in Christ.
Help us claim the richness of our glorious inheritance
in Christ, our shepherd.
Reveal to us your ways,
and guide us on right paths,
that we might bring the light of your love
to a world shrouded in shadow.
Bless this church with unity and strength,
that we may be Christ for the world.
For our shepherd rescues the perishing
and reclaims the lost and scattered
through those who follow as his sheep. Amen.

PROCLAMATION AND RESPONSE

PRAYER OF YEARNING *(Matthew 25)*
God of glory, we long to see your glory
in the world around us.
We yearn for the courage to meet another's eyes
when we find them in need.

We seek to be found faithful
> when we hear others cry out in distress.

Heal our sight when we fail to see you
> in our everyday lives.

Give us the vision to see others with compassion,
> that we might be your loving presence
> in the world. Amen.

~or~

PRAYER OF CONFESSION (Ezekiel 34, Matthew 25)
Loving Shepherd, we have not always reached out
> to the lost and scattered sheep of your flock.

We praise you with our lips,
> while averting our eyes from the hungry
> and those who lack shelter and warmth.

We lift our eyes to the starry heavens,
> while turning our gaze from the homeless
> and those who cannot help themselves.

Help us see others with the eyes of our shepherd,
> that we might be your loving presence
> in the world. Amen.

WORDS OF ASSURANCE (Ephesians 1)
There is immeasurable greatness in the power of God
> for those who believe.

There is unquenchable fire in the hearts of believers
> for those who have tasted God's hope.

In the name of Christ Jesus,
> we are offered fullness of life.

PASSING THE PEACE OF CHRIST (Ezekiel 34, Ephesians 1)
God loves us with a tenderness that can heal the deepest wounds in our souls. Christ offers us shelter in green pastures and leads us beside still waters. The Spirit offers us a peace that passes all understanding. Let our hearts rejoice this day, as we turn to our neighbors and share the peace of our shepherd.

INVITATION TO THE WORD (Matthew 25)
>Listen, our shepherd calls us here:
>>to feed one another,
>>to show compassion and love,
>>to offer comfort and mercy,
>>to give as freely as we have received.
>
>Listen, our shepherd is calling.

RESPONSE TO THE WORD (Matthew 25)
>Good Shepherd, help us be people of compassion.
>When we see a hungry child,
>>help us see your face.
>
>When we see a woman in rags,
>>help us see your dirty hands and feet.
>
>When we see a man sick or imprisoned,
>>help us see your need.
>
>When we hear your people cry,
>>help us see your tears.
>
>When we perceive mourning and loneliness,
>>help us perceive your presence,
>>>that our eyes may be enlightened,
>>>and our hearts of stone may be replaced
>>>>with hearts of flesh. Amen.

THANKSGIVING AND COMMUNION

INVITATION TO THE OFFERING (Psalm 100, Matthew 25)
>Enter God's gates with thanksgiving. Enter God's courtyard with praise. As sheep of God's fold, we have received goodness and grace from God's hand. Let us show our gratitude as we collect today's offering—an offering that continues Christ's work of mercy and compassion for all of God's lambs.

OFFERING PRAYER (Matthew 25)
Gentle Shepherd, may the gifts we bring this day:
be nourishment for a hungry world,
clothing and shelter for those in need,
and compassion for those who are hurting.
Bless these offerings,
that they may help those in need.
With gratitude, we pray. Amen.

SENDING FORTH

BENEDICTION (Ezekiel 34, Matthew 25)
Seek the lost and heal the injured.
**We will encourage the fainthearted
and strengthen the weak.**
Seek justice and love mercy.
**We will share God's justice
and offer Christ's grace.**
Go with God.

~or~

BENEDICTION (Psalm 100, Ephesians 1)
Leave this place with thankful hearts.
We will make a joyful noise to our God.
Bring shouts and laughter to the world.
We will sparkle with eyes enlightened.
Proclaim the tender mercies of our God.
We will share the good news with all.

Notes

November 26, 2026

Thanksgiving Day

Kristiane Smith

COLOR
White

SCRIPTURE READINGS
Deuteronomy 8:7-18; Psalm 65; 2 Corinthians 9:6-15; Luke 17:11-19

THEME IDEAS
Let us give thanks to the Lord our God! Today is a day set aside for thankfulness. Today's scriptures focus on praising God. In our Old Testament reading, our ancestors praise God for the abundance of the land, a gentle reminder not to take the life-giving resources God has provided for granted. In 2 Corinthians, there is a charge to be generous and share abundantly all that God has provided us. Luke focuses on the healed leaper who returned to honor Jesus with praise and thanksgiving for the miracle of health.

INVITATION AND GATHERING

CENTERING WORDS
In the quiet moments of this day, remember all the creator has given and give thanks.

CALL TO WORSHIP (Deuteronomy 8, Psalm 65)
Let us shout for joy and break out in song!
> Yet, even in the silence, God hears our praise.

In the mornings and evenings,
> we praise God's name in jubilant song
> and quiet prayer.

Our thankfulness can never outweigh God's abundance.
> Let us give thanks for all God has given.
> Praise the Lord!

OPENING PRAYER (Deuteronomy 8, Psalm 65)
Eternal One, we praise you for the lavish love
> you provide us.

Love experienced through the abundance of the earth,
> meets our every need.

As we gather this morning in worship,
> hear the thanks in our hearts and on our lips.

We praise your almighty name. Amen

PROCLAMATION AND RESPONSE

PRAYER OF YEARNING (Luke 17)
Here we are, Lord, speechless
> from your extravagant love for us.

You have given us everything we need to live life,
> and live it abundantly.

Yet sometimes, we are more like the nine
> who never return with simple thanks.

Let us be like the one who returns,
> lifting our arms in praise
>> and falling to our knees in reverence.

Enliven our spirits to go out and share the good news
> of our healings.

May we live a life of worship
> so that others may find their way back to you. Amen.

WORDS OF ASSURANCE *(Psalm 65, Corinthians 9)*
Bountiful blessings come in many different ways.
From the abundance of life-giving nutrients and water,
to places to rest our heads,
God provides out of love for God's creation.
May we respond with abundant thanks.

PASSING THE PEACE OF CHRIST
As you greet one another on this day of Thanks, share one thing you give thanks for God's work in their life.

RESPONSE TO THE WORD *(Deuteronomy 8, NRSV)*
As we celebrate the bounty of our lives, heed the word of God: "Take care that you do not forget the Lord your God, by failing to keep [God's] commandments. . . . Do not say to yourself, 'My power and the might of my own hand have gotten me this wealth.' But remember the Lord your God, for it is [God] who gives you power to get wealth. . . ." Let us remember who we are, whose we are, and where our blessings come from.

THANKSGIVING AND COMMUNION

INVITATION TO THE OFFERING *(2 Corinthians 9)*
God loves a cheerful giver. Since God has blessed us abundantly, may we return abundantly back to God through our thanks, praise, and gifts.

OFFERING PRAYER
As you have given to us,
may we now return to you.
Bless these gifts,
that they be used to share your gift
with our neighbors, far and near. Amen.

SENDING FORTH

BENEDICTION (2 Corinthians 9)
  As you leave this place,
    may your service to the community
    be blessed through your caring, sharing, and love.

Notes

November 29, 2026

First Sunday of Advent

Mary Scifres
Copyright © Mary Scifres

COLOR
Purple

SCRIPTURE READINGS
Isaiah 64:1-9; Psalm 80:1-7, 17-19; 1 Corinthians 1:3-9; Mark 13:24-37

THEME IDEAS
Actively awaiting Christ's arrival, we enter into this first week of Advent. Both Isaiah and Mark remind us that waiting is not to be passive, for passive waiting leads to idleness (Mark 13:36) and even sin (Isaiah 64:5-7). Challenging us to constant vigilance, today's scriptures encourage us to move past sleepwalking to constant readiness for what God is doing in the world.

INVITATION AND GATHERING

CENTERING WORDS (Isaiah 64)
May we listen deeply. May our ears perceive. May our eyes see that God is here, acting on our behalf, simply because we have arrived with waiting, expectant hearts.

CALL TO WORSHIP (1 Corinthians 1)
Thanking God for one another,
  we gather to worship and pray.
Richly blessed in everything we need,
  we gather in trust and hope.
Loved faithfully in Christ Jesus,
  we gather to sing and rejoice.

OPENING PRAYER (Isaiah 64, Mark 13)
Creator God, create us anew this Advent season.
Mold us to more firmly into your image.
Wake us to recognize your voice
  and listen deeply for your guidance.
Show us the signs that lead us closer to you,
  and help us bring your love to everyone we meet.
In Advent hope, we pray. Amen.

PROCLAMATION AND RESPONSE

PRAYER OF YEARNING (Isaiah 64, Psalm 80, Mark 13)
Shepherd of Israel, hear our prayers.
Hear the cries of our hearts
  and the confusion of our mind.
Hear the struggles of your creation,
  yearning to be healed and held by you.
Calm the chaos that swirls around us,
  that we might perceive your presence and guidance.
Heal the pain and worries that break us apart,
  and re-form us into the beautiful people
    you've created us to be.
In faith and hope, we pray. Amen.

WORDS OF ASSURANCE (Psalm 80, 1 Corinthians 1, Advent)
Christ's light is shining.
God's love is true.
And the Spirit is making us new.

NOVEMBER 29, 2026

PASSING THE PEACE OF CHRIST (1 Corinthians 1)
Grace and peace to you from Christ Jesus,
who is our redeemer and hope.
Grace and peace to you from Christ Jesus,
who is our redeemer and hope.
Let's share this grace and peace with one another.

INTRODUCTION TO THE WORD (Mark 13)
Wake up! This is not nap time. This is deep listening time.
Wake up, and listen for the word of God.

RESPONSE TO THE WORD (Isaiah 64, Mark 13)
God is still speaking.
May we listen deeply.
Christ is still teaching.
May our minds perceive.
The Spirit is constantly present.
May our spirits welcome God's Spirit:
to protect and guide us,
to form and mold us,
to shake us awake and point out new things,
to lead us to Christmas, to a new year,
and to a new world of love and justice.

THANKSGIVING AND COMMUNION

OFFERING PRAYER (Psalm 80, 1 Corinthians 1)
Gracious God, bless these gifts
to shine with the face of your love.
Bless our lives to reveal Christ's presence in the world.
Bless us to be faithful servants each and every day.
In the light of your love, we pray. Amen.

SENDING FORTH

BENEDICTION (Psalm 80, 1 Corinthians 1)
Revived and restored by God's love,
we will share holy love with the world.
With Christ's light to guide the way,
we will brighten the world with love.

Notes

December 6, 2026

Second Sunday of Advent

B. J. Beu
Copyright © B. J. Beu

COLOR
Purple

SCRIPTURE READINGS
Isaiah 40:1-11; Psalm 85:1-2, 8-13; 2 Peter 3:8-15a; Mark 1:1-8

THEME IDEAS

Advent is a time of waiting and longing for the day of righteousness and salvation promised by God. We are called to wait with patience and perseverance, even as we look forward to the time when faithful love and truth shall meet, and when righteousness and peace shall kiss. In our waiting, and in our preparing to receive the long awaited one, these scriptures invite us to slow down, embody peace, and share comfort in an impatient and harried world.

INVITATION AND GATHERING

CENTERING WORDS *(Psalm 85, 2 Peter 3, Mark 1)*
Christ is near. Yearn for the day when faithful love and truth shall meet, when righteousness and peace shall kiss. Prepare for the coming miracle.

CALL TO WORSHIP (Isaiah 40, Psalm 85)
Look! Faithful love and truth have met in this place.
> **Righteousness and peace have kissed.**

Listen! God is speaking words of hope.
> **Christ is calling us into God's flock.**

See! The glory of God shines all around us.
> **The love of Christ flows through our lives.**

Come! Let us worship.

OPENING PRAYER (Isaiah 40, Mark 1)
Shepherding God, lift us into your lap,
> and comfort our troubled minds.

Give us your rest and strengthen our weary bodies.
Guide us through this season of anticipation and hope,
> that we might lift our voices in laughter and song.

Make our paths straight,
> that we might move boldly forward
>> as we prepare for your arrival. Amen.

PROCLAMATION AND RESPONSE

PRAYER OF YEARNING (Isaiah 40, Psalm 85)
God of shepherding love,
> we need your guidance this day.

You proclaim that faithful love and truth have met,
> but we grow distracted waiting to see it.

You rejoice that righteousness and peace have kissed,
> but we yearn to believe it.

Breathe your grace into our lives,
> and give us the confidence to shout:
>> "Here is our God!" Amen.

WORDS OF ASSURANCE (Isaiah 40)
"Comfort, O comfort, my people," says our God.
We have served our term; our penalty is paid in full.
Rejoice in the good news.

DECEMBER 6, 2026

PASSING THE PEACE OF CHRIST (Psalm 85)
In Christ, faithful love and truth have met; righteousness and peace have kissed. May we, who eagerly await his arrival, share the blessings of Christ as we share his peace with one another this day.

INTRODUCTION TO THE WORD (Isaiah 40, Mark 1)
Prepare the way of the Lord.
Make straight the pathway for our God.
Prepare the way of the Lord.
Every valley will be raised up,
and every mountain will be brought low.
Prepare the way of the Lord.

RESPONSE TO THE WORD (Isaiah 40, 2 Peter 3, Mark 1)
Glorious God, Source of our hope,
   as we remember your promises of old,
      help us live into your coming future;
   as we reflect on the prophecies of advent,
      help us prepare for the coming of Christ;
   as we commit ourselves to the ways of peace,
      help us find joy in the journey. Amen.

THANKSGIVING AND COMMUNION

INVITATION TO THE OFFERING (Isaiah 40)
Grass may wither but God's word endures forever. Flowers may fade but the promises of Christ abide. In offering our gifts to a world in need, we transform wealth that fades into an indestructible currency of God's love for the world. Let us give freely and joyfully in the Spirit we find in Christ Jesus.

OFFERING PRAYER
You have sheltered us in your flock, O God.
You have gathered us in your arms
   and lifted us into your lap.

May the gifts we offer you this day,
reflect in some small measure,
the immense gratitude we feel
for the generosity of your love. Amen.

SENDING FORTH

BENEDICTION (Psalm 85, 2 Peter 3)
Christ is coming soon.
Love is all around.
Faithful love and truth have met.
Righteousness and peace have kissed.
We wait for the fullness of God's kingdom.
Christ is coming soon.
Love is on the way.

Notes

December 13, 2026

Third Sunday of Advent

Mary Scifres
Copyright © Mary Scifres

COLOR
Purple

SCRIPTURE READINGS
Isaiah 61:1-4, 8-11; Psalm 126; 1 Thessalonians 5:16-24; John 1:6-8, 19-28

THEME IDEAS
Today's scriptures point the way—the way of justice, the way of rejoicing (even in the midst of suffering), and the way of following the light. John the Baptist came to point to the way, not to be the way, for his cousin Jesus will be the way. Isaiah's prophesies point us toward justice, not to create justice, for God's followers are the ones called to create justice. Today's psalm and epistle point us on the path of joy, not to be the path of joy, for we are the travelers who blaze the trail of joy. Pointing the way, today's scriptures invite us to journey on the way, not just to Advent, but to a year of traveling the way with Christ the Way.

INVITATION AND GATHERING

CENTERING WORDS *(Isaiah 61, Psalm 126,*
1 Thessalonians 5, John 1)
May joy fill our hearts; may justice guide our days; and may we walk in the light of Christ's love.

CALL TO WORSHIP *(Isaiah 61, John 1)*
A voice cries in the darkest wilderness:
Prepare the way, light is ahead!
A voice of love calls in our darkest days:
Hear the good news, comfort for all.
The voice of God has called us here.
We are ready and waiting, listening for hope.

OPENING PRAYER or PRAYER OF YEARNING *(Isaiah 61)*
God of Advent and Christmas,
 help us embrace both seasons,
  even as they intermingle in our world.
Help us wait patiently, listen quietly,
 and anticipate hopefully.
Help us also to celebrate Christmas,
 even before it arrives—
 with good news and good help
  for the poor and brokenhearted,
 with comfort and support for the grieving,
 and with love for the lost and alone.
Celebrate with us, O God,
 by guiding our days with grace
  and by leading our lives with love. Amen.

PROCLAMATION AND RESPONSE

PRAYER OF YEARNING *(Isaiah 61, Psalm 126,*
1 Thessalonians 5, John 1)
Just and joyous God, make straight the crooked paths of our lives.

Guide us back to your way when we wander off course.
Breathe peace when turmoil and trouble haunt our lives.
Show us the truth of your salvation with love and grace,
    and help us to shine with the salvation of love
        and grace for all to see.
For what better candlelight is there
    than that of love and grace?

WORDS OF ASSURANCE (John 1, John 8:12, Matthew 5:14)

You are the light of the world,
    led by the light of the world, Christ Jesus.
Shine with this truth.

PASSING THE PEACE OF CHRIST (John 1, 1 Thessalonians 5, Ephesians 2)

May you know the light of peace.
May you be the light of peace.
For Christ is our peace.

INTRODUCTION TO THE WORD (John 1)

Look and listen, for the light of God shines through the Word of God. May we sense the light in today's reading and message.

RESPONSE TO THE WORD (Isaiah 61)

May we be people of God's Holy Spirit:
    bringing good news,
healing and helping,
    advocating and liberating,
comforting and consoling,
    loving and listening,
singing and rejoicing.
    May we be people of God's Holy Spirit.

THANKSGIVING AND COMMUNION

INVITATION TO THE OFFERING (John 1, 1 Thessalonians 5, Ephesians 2)
May we offer our gifts as Christ's light and peace to the world.

OFFERING PRAYER (John 1, John 8, Matthew 5)
Light of the world, shine through the gifts
   we return to you now.
Shine through our lives, and shine in your world,
   that all may be led by the light of your love
      and grace. Amen.

SENDING FORTH

BENEDICTION
May joy fill our hearts.
May justice guide our days.
And may we walk in the light of Christ's love.

DECEMBER 13, 2026

Notes

December 20, 2026

Fourth Sunday of Advent
Mary Petrina Boyd

COLOR
Purple

SCRIPTURE READINGS
2 Samuel 7:1-11, 16; Luke 1:46b-55; Romans 16:25-27; Luke 1:26-38

THEME IDEAS
There is great mystery here. God refused to dwell in a temple but comes to dwell in the body of a young woman. God's ways turn expectations upside down, bringing down the powerful while lifting up the lowly. This is a time of rejoicing, as we prepare for the coming of Christ.

INVITATION AND GATHERING

CENTERING WORDS (Luke 1)
God entered the world in a new way. God joined forces with an ordinary young woman to bring forth new life and hope for all creation.

~or~

DECEMBER 20, 2026

CENTERING WORDS *(2 Samuel 7)*
God is not confined to churches or holy places. God is utterly free, traveling beside us wherever we go.

CALL TO WORSHIP *(Romans 16)*
God alone is wise.
Glory be to God!
This is the good news.
Glory be to God!
Jesus comes to us.
Glory be to God!

~or~

CALL TO WORSHIP *(Luke 1)*
God comes to us.
Let us rejoice!
God's mercy is for everyone.
God pulls down the mighty.
God lifts up the lowly
God feeds the hungry.
God sends the rich away.
God comes to our aid.
God comes to us.
Let us rejoice!

OPENING PRAYER *(Luke 1)*
Holy One, you enter our world with promise and hope.
You invite us into lives of courage and compassion,
    carrying your love into all the world.
Give us ears to hear your invitation
    and hearts willing to embark on new adventures.
As Mary brought Jesus into the world,
    may we carry the love of Jesus into the world today.
Amen.

PROCLAMATION AND RESPONSE

**PRAYER OF CONFESSION or PRAYER OF YEARNING
(2 Samuel 7)**

    We would tie you down, O God.
    We want to be assured that you are in a specific place,
        where we can always find you.
    We would like to limit you
        to fit into our human understanding.
    You, Holy One, are the great mystery,
        beyond human comprehension.
    Our human thoughts cannot fully comprehend
        your nature.
    Yet you chose us, provide for us, shelter us.
    You walk beside us.
    In so many ways you bless us.
    Help us expand our hearts,
        let go of a need to fully understand,
            and dare to simply encounter you as you are,
                incomprehensible yet present. Amen.

~or~

PRAYER OF YEARNING (Luke 1)

    O God you call us to follow you
        on adventures we can't imagine.
    We're afraid.
    We don't understand what might happen.
    We're sure that we aren't capable of what you ask.
    Teach us to trust your love.
    Even when we don't feel able or worthy,
        you are God and you can use ordinary people
            to do extraordinary things.
    Bring forth new life within us.
    We know that nothing is impossible with you. Amen.

WORDS OF ASSURANCE *(Luke 1)*
The angel told Mary, "Rejoice, favored one!
  The Lord is with you!"
Let us rejoice this day, for indeed, God is with us!

~or~

WORDS OF ASSURANCE *(Luke 1)*
Truly God shows mercy to everyone!

PASSING THE PEACE OF CHRIST *(Luke 1)*
Gabriel greeted Mary, "Rejoice, favored one! The Lord is with you." Rejoice as you greet one another remembering that the Lord is with you.

PRAYER OF PREPARATION *(Luke 1)*
Holy one, center our hearts in your mystery and love,
  that we may hear your word today.
Give us wisdom to hear and understand
  the depth of your truth.
Strengthen our spirits,
  that we may find courage to respond to your call.
Amen.

RESPONSE TO THE WORD *(Luke 1)*
O God, the angel Gabriel came to Mary
  interrupting her life, calling her on a new adventure.
You come to us still, seeing possibilities for our world
  we can't image.
May we have the courage to hear you and to respond,
  "Let it be with each of us, just as you have said."
Amen.

LITANY *(Luke 1:46b-55, CEB adapted)*
And Mary said, In the depths of who I am I rejoice in you,
O God my savior.
  **You have looked with favor on the low status
  of your servant.**

Look! From now on, everyone will consider me
highly favored because you, the mighty one,
have done great things for me.
> **Holy is your name, O God.**
You show mercy to everyone,
> **from one generation to the next,**
> **all who honors you as God.**
You have shown strength with your arm.
> **You have scattered those with arrogant thoughts**
> **and proud inclinations.**
You have pulled down the powerful from their thrones
and lifted up the lowly.
> **You have filled the hungry with good things**
> **and sent the rich away empty-handed.**
You have come to the aid of your servant Israel,
remembering your mercy,
> **just as you promised to our ancestors,**
> **to Abraham and to Abraham's descendants forever."**

THANKSGIVING AND COMMUNION

INVITATION TO THE OFFERING (Luke 1)

Mary sang of God's generous love, a love that lifts up the lowly and feeds the hungry. Let us share this generous spirit as we bring our gifts today.

OFFERING PRAYER (Luke 1)

Generous and giving God, you provide all that we need.
You care for us.
Grateful for your abiding presence in our lives,
> we offer these gifts to you.
May they fill the hungry with good things,
> as we care for our neighbors.
We offer ourselves to you.
Use us for your work in the world. Amen.

DECEMBER 20, 2026

SENDING FORTH

BENEDICTION (2 Samuel 7, Romans 16)
Go forth, knowing that God goes with you.
May the Holy Spirit guide your steps
and may Jesus Christ strengthen you always.

Notes

December 24, 2026

Christmas Eve

Karen Clark Ristine

COLOR
White

SCRIPTURE READINGS
Isaiah 9:2-7; Psalm 96; Titus 2:11-14; Luke 2:1-20

THEME IDEAS
Christmas Eve celebrates the beginning of the Christian story and the continuation of the creation story. The culmination of the Christmas Eve story comes on Easter Sunday. And the continuation comes in how we live our lives. This is our origin story as people of faith. This night's scriptures are familiar to many, whether they have heard them in lessons and carols on Christmas Eve, or in the voice of Linus van Pelt. As you mark Christmas Eve in the tradition of your faith community, may you soar with the Spirit as you lead this holy night.

INVITATION AND GATHERING

CENTERING WORDS (Luke 2, "O Holy Night")
"O holy night! the stars are brightly shining; It is the night of the dear Savior's birth."

DECEMBER 24, 2026

CALL TO WORSHIP (Luke 2)
    Christ is born!
    Christ is born, indeed!
    Alleluia!

OPENING PRAYER (Luke 2)
    Gracious and loving Creator, on this holy night,
        we celebrate the birth of Jesus and welcome him
            as your greatest example of how you love us.
    Open our hearts anew to the miracle of this birth,
        the depth of this love, and the wonder of this night.
    Amen.

PROCLAMATION AND RESPONSE

PRAYER OF YEARNING (Titus 2, Luke 2)
    Precious Lord Jesus, this night you come to us
        as an infant in a manger.
    We long to offer you the gift of our hearts, our minds,
        and our lives.
    Thank you for your gift of presence with us.
    We yearn to follow you in ways that lead to life
        and to hope, love and peace for all the world. Amen.

WORDS OF ASSURANCE (Isaiah 9:2-7, NRSV)
    "The people who walked in darkness have seen a great light; those who lived in a land of deep darkness—on them light has shined. . . . For a child has been born for us, a son given to us; authority rests upon his shoulders; and he is named Wonderful Counselor, Mighty God, Everlasting Father, Prince of Peace."

PASSING THE PEACE OF CHRIST (Isaiah 9, Luke 2:10, NRSV/KJV)
    This holy night, we will pass the light of Christ to one another, and as we do, we receive for ourselves the words of the angels to the shepherds: "Fear not, for behold I bring

you good tidings of great joy which shall be to all people."
As the light of Christ increases and brightens in this sanctuary this night, may we each take this light into our lives and into the world.

The peace and light of Christ be with you all.
And also with you.

RESPONSE TO THE WORD *(Isaiah 9, Psalm 96, Luke 2)*
Infant Jesus, this night, we sing and bless
> your many names.
Like the shepherds at the cradle, we glorify God.
Like your mother, Mary, we treasure this night
> and ponder in our hearts the miracle of your birth,
> > your life, your ministry, and your resurrection.

THANKSGIVING AND COMMUNION

OFFERING PRAYER *(Luke 2)*
In response to the gift of the amazing love
> you offer this night, we offer ourselves—
> > all that we are, all that we can be—
> > > to share Christ's love with others. Amen.

SENDING FORTH

BENEDICTION
Go now from this liminal place,
> where we have set time aside,
> > to return to the cradle of the infant Jesus.
Go into the night, into your lives.
In the name of the Creator, the Christ and the Spirit:
> Take this light of Christ into the world
> > and help it grow.

Notes

December 27, 2026

First Sunday after Christmas
Kristiane Smith

COLOR
White

SCRIPTURE READINGS
Isaiah 61:10–62:3; Psalm 148; Galatians 4:4-7; Luke 2:22-40

THEME IDEAS

After a busy advent season, perhaps a hymn sing is in order on this Sunday. Today's readings present us with imagery of praise, worship, incarnation, and the righteousness of Christ. Isaiah proclaims, "I surely rejoice in the Lord; my heart is joyful because of my God" (Isaiah 61:10a, CEB). "All Hail the Power of Jesus' Name" shares the foretelling of Jesus' birth in Isaiah's song, "O seed of Israel's chosen race" (v. 2). In Psalm 148, we hear the exclamations of joy through creation's song. We can't help but sing along with *heaven and nature* as we sing "Joy to the World." While our epistle today does not directly mention Jesus' birth, Paul does write of the incarnation, "But when the fulfillment of the time came, God sent his Son, born through a woman" (Galatians 4:4a). We hear this beautiful imagery in Charles Wesley's "Hark the Herald Angels Sing." Our Gospel reading finds Mary and Joseph faithfully arriving at the temple to present Jesus. We witness Simone and the prophet Anna's response to encountering Jesus (Luke 1:38). May we always remember to "Go Tell it On the Mountain, that Jesus Christ is Born."

INVITATION AND GATHERING

CENTERING WORDS
The baby King is with us. Keep sharing the joy with others.

CALL TO WORSHIP (Psalm 148)
Joy to the World!
Praise the Lord from heaven.
Let Earth receive her King.
Let all creation, praise God!
Every heart prepare him room.
Praise the Lord!

OPENING PRAYER (Psalm 48, Luke 2)
All creation sings your name, Lord.
We bow at the manger and fall to our knees
    at the temple.
As we gather in this holy space,
    fill our hearts with unending joy.
May holy songs escape our lips in worship to you.
Amen.

PROCLAMATION AND RESPONSE

PRAYER OF YEARNING (Psalm 48, Luke 2)
When the lights dimmed as we sang "Silent Night,"
    our hearts wondered, what's next?
Would we return, lives unchanged,
    to a world that needs your light more than ever?
This world needs our joy more than ever,
    and you charge each of us to go and share it.

Help us keep our candles lit,
> that the world might experience your light and love.
Fill us with the awe of Simon
> and the excitement of Anna,
>> that your presence might touch our songs.
In the mighty name of Jesus, we pray. Amen.

WORDS OF ASSURANCE (Luke 2)
The revelation is unfolding, and peace has come.
The light of the world is in our midst.

RESPONSE TO THE WORD (Luke 2)
May we experience Jesus through the eyes of Simeon
> and the faith of Anna.
May we rest with contentment
> that we have been in the presence of the Holy One.
May we go forth with exaltation to proclaim his arrival.

THANKSGIVING AND COMMUNION

INVITATION TO THE OFFERING (Galatians 4, Luke 2)
God has adopted us into God's kinship. As children of God, we are not only heirs but also receive responsibility for spreading his message and word. In giving our tithes and offerings, we continue God's work.

OFFERING PRAYER
Redeeming God, thank you for loving us.
Take these offerings as a token of our gratitude
> for all you have done.
Multiply these gifts and them send them into the world
> to share blessings with all. Amen.

DECEMBER 27, 2026

SENDING FORTH

BENEDICTION
    Just as we sang for joy, celebrated in community,
        and worshiped together,
        let us depart with voices full of song,
        proclaiming from every mountain
        that Jesus Christ is born.

Notes

Contributors

B. J. Beu is a retired local church pastor, spiritual director, and executive coach. B. J. lives in Laguna Beach, California, with his wife, Mary, and enjoys spending time with their son, Michael Beu, and his fiancé, April Fisher.

Michael Beu is a professional film editor who works with Five Star Events. He also serves as worship editor for several churches in California. Find out more at www.element productions.net.

Mary Petrina Boyd is pastor of Marysville United Methodist Church, northeast of Seattle. She spends alternating summers working as an archaeologist in Jordan.

Anna Crews Camphouse is a nurse, pastor, counselor, mom, and co-journeyer with those working to build hope and goodness in the world.

Lisa Ann Moss Degrenia brings over thirty years of ministry experience as a church music director and pastor to this project. She currently serves as the senior pastor of Coronado Community United Methodist Church in New Smyrna Beach, Florida. For more of her prayer resources, go to www.revlisad.com.

Karin Ellis is a United Methodist pastor who lives with her husband and children in La Cañada, California. She enjoys writing liturgy for worship and children's stories.

CONTRIBUTORS

Rebecca J. Kruger Gaudino, a United Church of Christ minister in Portland, Oregon, teaches biblical studies and theology at the University of Portland and also writes for the Church.

Amy B. Hunter is a religious educator and spiritual director in Lowell, Massachussetts. She is an Episcopal layperson who loves liturgy and the occasional opportunity to preach.

Kirsten Linford serves as senior minister of Westwood Hills Congregational (UCC) church and preschool in Los Angeles. She shares her life with her young daughter, Riley, and their golden retriever, Seamus. Ecumenism is in her blood. Pastoring and parenting with a UCC head and a Disciples of Christ heart, she is delighted to be writing for a United Methodist publishing house.

Karen Clark Ristine worked for more than twenty years as a newspaper reporter and editor in Oakland, Dallas, and San Diego before answering a call to ordained ministry in The United Methodist Church. She takes great joy when her love of words combines with her love of The Word. She is married to Dr. Marcia McFee and lives in Kansas City, Missouri. Her son Ryan, a musician and music educator, teaches in Santa Rosa, California.

Mary J. Scifres is a retired United Methodist pastor serving as a leadership coach, consultant, and author. Learn more at www.maryscifres.com.

LeighAnn Shaw is an ordained elder in the United Methodist Church, who lives in Carlsbad, California. She loves writing and exploring and advocating for those without a voice.

Kristiane Smith is a United Methodist pastor serving in Southern California. Her passions include creative writing, music, hanging out with her husband and three teens, and helping others examine and make sense of their faith journey.

CONTRIBUTORS

Leigh Anne Taylor walks alongside her husband, Hugh, and their five children and four grandchildren as a blessed "LaLa" among the clergy and churches of the Mountain View District in south central Virginia as Director of Connecting Ministries. She loves learning about the Enneagram of the Soul and spiritual practices.

Scripture Index

Old Testament

Genesis
1:1–2:4a 119
2:15-17; 3:1-7 41
12:1-4a 45
12:1-9 123
18:1-15 128
21:8-21 133
22:1-14 138
24:34-38, 42-49, 58-67 142
25:19-34 148
28:10-19a 152
29:15-28 157
32:22-31 162
37:1-4, 12-28 167
45:1-15 173

Exodus
1:8–2:10 177
3:1-15 182
12:1-14 188
12:1-4, (5-10) 11-14 68
14:19-31 194
15:1b-11, 20-21 194
16:2-15 199
17:1-7 .... 50, 203
20:1-4, 7-9, 12-20 207
24:12-18 31
32:1-14 212
33:12-23 216

Deuteronomy
8:7-18 243
34:1-12 220

Joshua
24:1-3a, 14-25 228

Judges
4:1-7 232

1 Samuel
16:1-13 54

2 Samuel
7:1-11, 16 260

Psalms
8 119
13 138
15 21
16 84
17:1-7, 15 162
19 207
22 74
23 .... 54, 94
27:1, 4-9 16
29 6
31:1-5, 15-16 99
31:9-16 63
32 41
33:1-12 123
34:1-10, 22 224
40:1-11 11
45:10-17 142
47 109
51:1-17 36
65 243
66:8-20 104

SCRIPTURE INDEX

Psalms (continued)
68:1-10, 32-35 109
72:1-7, 10-14 1
78:1-4, 12-16 203
78:1-7 228
80:1-7, 17-19 247
85:1-2, 8-13 251
86:1-10, 16-17 133
90:1-6, 13-17 220
95 50
96 266
99 .... 31, 216
100 237
104:24-34, 35b 114
105:1-6, 16-22, 45b 167
105:1-6, 23-26, 45b 182
105:1-6, 37-45 199
105:1-11, 45b 157
106:1-6, 19-23 212
112:1-9 (10) 26
116:1-2, 12-19 .... 68, 128
116:1-4, 12-19 89
118:1-2, 14-24 78
118:1-2, 19-29 63
119:105-112 148
121 45
123 232
124 177

126 255
130 58
133 173
139:1-12, 23-24 152
148 270
149 188

Isaiah
9:1-4 16
9:2-7 266
40:1-11 251
42:1-9 6
49:1-7 11
50:4-9a 63
52:13–53:12 74
58:1-9a (9b-12) 26
60:1-6 1
61:1-4, 8-11 255
61:10–62:3 270
64:1-9 247

Ezekiel
34:11-16, 20-24 237
37:1-14 58

Joel
2:1-2, 12-17 36

Micah
6:1-8 21

New Testament

Matthew
2:1-12 1
3:13-17 6
4:1-11 41
4:12-23 16
5:1-12 .... 21, 224
5:13-20 26

6:1-6, 16-21 36
9:9-13, 18-26 123
9:35–10:8 (9-23) 128
10:24-39 133
10:40-42 138
11:16-19, 25-30 142
13:1-9, 18-23 148

SCRIPTURE INDEX

13:24-30, 36-43 152
13:31-33, 44-52 157
14:13-21 162
14:22-33 167
15:(10-20) 21-28 173
16:13-20 177
16:21-28 182
17:1-9 31
18:15-20 188
18:21-35 194
20:1-16 199
21:1-11 63
21:23-32 203
21:33-46 207
22:1-14 212
22:15-22 216
22:34-46 220
25:1-13 228
25:14-30 232
25:31-46 237
26:14–27:66 63
27:11-54 63
28:1-10 78
28:16-20 119

Mark
1:1-8 251
13:24-37 247

Luke
1:26-38 260
1:46b-55 260
2:1-20 266
2:22-40 270
17:11-19 243
24:13-35 89
24:44-53 109

John
1:6-8, 19-28 255
1:29-42 11

3:1-17 45
4:5-42 50
7:37-39 114
9:1-41 54
10:1-10 94
11:1-45 58
13:1-17, 31b-35 68
14:1-14 99
14:15-21 104
17:1-11 109
18:1–19:42 74
20:1-18 78
20:19-31 84

Acts
1:1-11 109
1:6-14 109
2:1-21 114
2:14a, 22-32 84
2:14a, 36-41 89
2:42-47 94
7:55-60 99
10:34-43 .... 6, 78
17:22-31 104

Romans
4:1-5, 13-17 45
4:13-25 123
5:1-8 128
5:1-11 50
5:12-19 41
6:1b-11 133
6:12-23 138
7:15-25a 142
8:1-11 148
8:6-11 58
8:12-25 152
8:26-39 157
9:1-5 162
10:5-15 167
11:1-2a, 29-32 173

SCRIPTURE INDEX

Romans (continued)
12:1-8 177
12:9-21 182
13:8-14 188
14:1-12 194
16:25-27 260

1 Corinthians
1:1-9 11
1:3-9 247
1:10-18 16
1:18-31 21
2:1-12 (13-16) 26
11:23-26 68
12:3b-13 114

2 Corinthians
5:20b–6:10 36
9:6-15 243
13:11-13 119

Galatians
4:4-7 270

Ephesians
1:15-23 .... 109, 237
3:1-12 1
5:8-14 54

Philippians
1:21-30 199
2:1-13 203
2:5-11 63
3:4b-14 207
4:1-9 212

Colossians
3:1-4 78

1 Thessalonians
1:1-10 216
2:1-8 220
4:13-18 228
5:1-11 232
5:16-24 255

Titus
2:11-14 266

Hebrews
4:14-16, 5:7-9
10:16-25 74

1 Peter
1:3-9 84
1:17-23 89
2:2-10 99
2:19-25 94
3:13-22 104
4:12-14, 5:6-11 109

2 Peter
1:16-21 31
3:8-15a 251

1 John
3:1-3 224

Revelation
7:9-17 224

A new planning tool for worship & preaching!

Call & Response: The Abingdon Guidebook for Worship and Preaching, Year A, 2025-2026

An essential source of planning throughout the Christian Year

A trustworthy partner for any pastor, worship planner, laity or staff involved in planning worship services or sermons for their church, *Call & Response* by R. DeAndre Johnson is structured around the Christian calendar. It is rich with resources for Advent, Lent, Pentecost, and the other seasons and special days of the liturgical year.

Each section provides the full text of all the calls to worship, responsive readings, offering invitations, benedictions, and other prayers and liturgies needed for worship services all year long.

Beginning with Advent and moving through the Christian Year, the resource includes sermon development prompts based on thematic and lectionary approaches. Throughout, worship practitioners of every experience level will find sidebars with instructive material related to the meaning, history, and logistics.

Features a wide and varied pool of contributor voices, material from ancient and contemporary sources, as well as suggestions for engaging all generations together in worship.

from

For more information, call 800.672.1789
or visit cokesbury.com/Call-Response

www.ingramcontent.com/pod-product-compliance
Lightning Source LLC
Chambersburg PA
CBHW011748220426
43669CB00020B/2947